TEX SAMPLE

HARD LIVING PEOPLE & MAINSTREAM CHRISTIANS

ABINGDON PRESS / Nashville

HARD LIVING PEOPLE AND MAINSTREAM CHRISTIANS

This book is printed on recycled, acid-free paper.

Library of Congress Cataloging-in-Publication Data

Sample, Tex.
    Hard living people and mainstream Christians/Tex Sample.
        p.   cm.
    Includes bibliographical references and index.
    ISBN 0-687-17931-9 (acid-free paper)
    1. Church work with the homeless. 2. Church work with narcotic addicts. 3. Homeless persons. 4. Narcotic addicts. I. Title.
BV4456.S26   1993
259'.08'694—dc20   92-40682
                                                                  CIP

Every effort has been made by the author to secure permission from persons who are identified by name and quoted directly or described indirectly in this book. Names and specific identifying information for other persons have been modified at the discretion of the author to protect privacy.

To
Saint Paul School of Theology

CONTENTS

PART TWO

WHAT TO DO

CONTENTS

ACKNOWLEDGMENTS

No one writes a manuscript alone, and the scope of my indebtedness exceeds my capacity to express appreciation fully. Furthermore, inevitably one cannot name all the persons who contributed an insight, a question, a feeling, a sensibility, a resource, or a name. Still, some must be mentioned just so minimal justice can be done.

I am indebted to Saint Paul School of Theology, its trustees, administration, and faculty for the sabbatical leave I received in the spring of 1992 when the last phase of the research and the first draft of the manuscript were done. I am especially indebted to Bishop W. T. Handy, Jr., chair of the trustees, President Lovett H. Weems, Jr., and Academic Dean Judith Orr for their encouragement and support.

A number of people read the manuscript and made unusually helpful suggestions: Rexine Bryant, Paul K. Deats, Jr., Eugene L. Lowry, and Emilie M. Townes. Each of these persons made genuine contributions that improved the manuscript. I wish my response to their suggestions was as constructive as their contributions. It is I and not they who must finally be responsible for what is here. I have always been blessed with better friends than I deserved.

Leila Disburg and Peggy Michael-Rush worked faithfully on transcribing the interviews with hard living people. Kathryn Boren obtained permission from the pastors to quote them as reported herein. I do not know how I could have written this without their help.

Kathleen Campbell has worked with me as a research assistant for years now. Her meticulous, intelligent, and good-humored efforts are beyond anything I could say to convey the extent of her gifts and my indebtedness.

Margaret Kohl is secretary to the faculty at Saint Paul, and, yet, with all her responsibilities she typed and retyped these lines through several drafts. Her skill, her helpful questions, and her ongoing commentary went well beyond word processing alone. She made substantive impact on the book.

Working with Paul Franklyn of Abingdon Press has been a pleasure. He is a thoughtful and perceptive editor. His suggestions, especially on a structural change, significantly improved the text. I appreciate his patient attention and care.

The class at Saint Paul on *Mainline Churches and U.S. Lifestyles* carried out one of two basic research tasks in their interviews of the sixty-five hard living people who appear here. The transcriptions of their interviews, really of their listening to hard living people tell their life stories, were even better than I thought they would be, and I knew from the reports in class that they had done fine work. It is one more significant instance of the gifts that the wonderful students of Saint Paul have made to my life. One of my greatest joys has been to teach and work with them for the past twenty-five years.

Without the hard living people who agreed to talk with us, who were candid and forthright, and who shared both pain and laughter, this book could not have been written. I am deeply obligated to them. I hope these pages will lead to a more humane appreciation for and interest in them and their stories. As we promised, we have protected their anonymity by using other names and changing nonessential details in their stories.

The pastors and religious leaders whom I interviewed deserve special thanks and gratitude. What I had not anticipated was how touched and moved I would be by their commitment, their faith, and the dedication that they brought to their work. My indebtedness to them, like that to the hard living goes beyond the concerns of the book. They have affected my life in a lasting way.

Finally, I have been in love with Peggy Sample for thirty-seven years and married to her for thirty-five. She is quite simply the finest person I have ever known. Her life blesses everything I do.

HARD LIVING

If you cannot stand four-letter words, do not read this book. The book is full of such language, and there is a very good reason. The focus here is a largely unchurched group of United States Americans who do not typically attend worship or other congregational programs. In fact, many of them hate the church, and some with plenty of cause. I call them hard living people, which I will define more carefully in chapter 1. They tend to be a disreputable bunch, and their conversation makes enormous use of primal Anglo-Saxon language. Because I believe language is basic to the structuring of social and cultural "reality," one cannot take away the language of hard living people without stealing away or, at least, distorting the particularities of their lives. The church is too put off by such things anyhow. More than that, churches do not have significant ministries *with* the hard living; these are usually, when churches have them, ministries *to* the hard living in the form of food, clothing, shelter, and other basic needs. We need to move closer, and this book is concerned precisely with how mainstream Christians can move into ministry and mission *with* the hard living.

Mac Charles Jones is the senior pastor of the St. Stephen's Baptist Church, a large prestigious African American congregation in Kansas City, Missouri. He and I coincidentally wound up as speakers to a Disciples Conference in Indianapo-

lis. I spoke in the morning, and he addressed an outdoor
gathering for peace and justice at a park in the center of the
city, which closed the meeting.

After Mac greeted well-wishers who expressed gratitude for
a rousing speech, we had less than forty-five minutes to catch
an airplane at an airport which, with traffic, was located at
least thirty minutes away. We had to go.

As we walked along a sidewalk to a waiting taxi, I spotted a
street person who had seen us and was coming straight for us.
He was tousled, bleary-eyed, and seemed to be in the sobering
up stage of a stiff drunk. Wearing the baggy slacks and plaid
shirt of a thrift store—all in wrinkled disarray—he also had on
a dark gray, well-traveled overcoat that appeared to be stained
with drink, vestiges of food, and some evidence of recent
nausea. He was an African American, and I simply said to
myself, *I want to see how Mac handles this,* so I slowed a half step
as Mac moved directly into the path of the man.

"Brother," said Mac, "have you eaten lately?"

"No, Reverend, I haven't and if you could just spare a little
change. It would . . .

"No, Brother, you need to eat something. You need some
food," interrupted Mac. "You come on and get in our cab, and
we'll take you down the street to a place where we can get you
something to eat."

The three of us loaded into the cab, stopped at a fast food
place, where Mac and I bought him a five dollar meal, and we
left him there to reach our plane successfully.

I have thought about this story many times since it happened. I
remember how differently Mac treated the man I wanted to avoid.
You see, to me he was a wino; to Mac he was a brother.

This book is about people like that man. They are not all
African American. They are black, brown, white, gold, and
red. They are women, too. Some are urban, some rural. Not all
of them are homeless by any means, not all of them are poor,
but most are. By *hard living* I mean people who have abused
alcohol and other drugs, have a history of violence either as a
perpetrator or a victim or both, have uneven employment,

have struggled with household or family relations, and tend to be politically alienated. They are looked down on as street people, poor white trash, homeless, disreputable, drunks, addicts, winos, skid row bums, hobos, trashy women, sluts, bikers, vagabonds, the underclass, the ne'er-do-wells, the lazy, the no-goods, and on and on.

These are the people who will often come to a church or a charitable agency to get food, clothing, medical care, legal services, whatever, but there is perhaps no group so hard for the church to reach in order to involve them in the active life of the congregation. While many churches serve them, few include them in the participating membership of the community of faith. They are seen as winos, or trash, or street people, or something else, but not as brothers and sisters.

One of the reasons for this view is that they are often not the kind of persons that we relate to. Their drinking and drugging, their hygiene, their life-styles, their protest of respectability and middle class norms, their disdain for established church life, their unwillingness to participate in church or any other group except on their terms, their resourceful use of the age-old hustle and con, their occasional violence, their vulgarity, their plain four-letter talk, their unrestrained use of obscene gestures and raucous humor, their often loud and unabashed approach to conflict, their quick condemnation of the church as hypocritical and self-serving: these are but a few of the problems as perceived by respectable mainstream church-going people. The problem is that great truth can be found in these depictions, even though they do not characterize them all. Sometimes, too, which can be worse, they get saved, or baptized in the Spirit, and they join some "insufferable" Pentecostal or fundamentalist congregation from whence they then emerge as the true believers of the one and only righteous church with an absolute morality and an assured but exclusive route to heaven.

No wonder such people are not only not sought out but avoided by churches. I want to know more about them. The opportunity came when I taught a course on Mainline

Churches and U.S. Lifestyles at Saint Paul School of Theology in the spring of 1991. With a class of twenty-three students the project of the course became an assignment for each student to "interview" three hard living people. We had found that interviews did not work well, so we changed the format by asking hard living people simply to tell us their life stories. This was unusually effective. We had a few things we especially wanted to know—like their relationship to the church, their view of God, family life, work experience, and so on—but we tried to ask about these only if they did not come up naturally in the course of telling their stories. We knew that storytelling was indigenous to hard living people, and we were not disappointed with the candor, the feeling, and the often revealing detail that they shared. Promising each of them anonymity in our research, all of the names have been changed along with unessential details in the stories to protect their identities. We wound up with sixty-five usable narratives which transcribed into about four hundred pages of text. Chapters 2 through 4 report on these narratives in terms of their family lives, relations between men and women, the drug world, their views of the church, their understanding of God and spirituality, and a discussion of an issue of control in their relation or lack of it to the church, which will occupy significant attention throughout the book.

The hard living people we interview are found in homeless shelters, detox centers, urban ministry settings, local apartments and residences, and honky-tonks in six midwestern cities.

Very few people we interview have any active relationship to a church. I am not surprised because I have been looking for four years to find churches across the United States that not only serve the hard living with food, clothing, and shelter—as important as that is—but also churches that are able to include them in active congregational life. More than that, I want to find *mainline* churches with mainstream Christians that are inclusive of them.

I once addressed a group of fifty mainstream pastors from a

good-sized denomination. At one point I told them of my research and asked if any of their churches included hard living people.

"You are asking the wrong denomination. Those are not our people."

That comment so bothered me that I left more determined than ever to find at least *some* mainstream churches who include the hard living. You see, I utterly detest the homogeneity principle, an unfaithful assertion which observes that churches will typically appeal to the same kind of people if they expect to grow and prosper. I do not doubt that it works, but so do orgies. The principle does not faithfully reflect the nature of the church as revealed to us at Pentecost where that diversity of people from all over the known world came together and suddenly by the power of the Spirit began to understand one another and to be understood.

I found forty pastors and a few other religious leaders who worked in such congregations. I interviewed thirty of them by phone and ten others in person. Of special interest were the things that enabled their churches to reach and incorporate the hard living. What were the orientations of these pastors? How did they view the hard living in terms of their own faith commitments? What was effective in working with them? What forms of worship, of preaching, of congregational life, of education, of leadership? How did they provide the services so that these did not become demeaning charity? How had these pastors done indigenous ministry? What were the practices of hard living people themselves, and how were these incorporated into the life and the ministry of the church? How did they get started? What kind of trouble and conflict occurred when the hard living joined the church? How did they work with it? What would they do differently? What advice or wisdom did they have to share? Over and over again, I asked how they worked with the problem of control that surfaced in our interviews with the hard living? And, finally, how had they attempted to deal with systemic issues, with the structured social inequality of poverty? How had they attempted to do social change, to do organizing, to work for social justice? The responses of the pastors and religious leaders to these questions are discussed in chapters 6 through 10.

LANGUAGE AND CONCEPTS

In this book I attempt to stay away from theory, sociological concepts, and reinterpretations of the reports of both the hard living and the pastors. Obviously *any* treatment of this kind *is* an interpretation, but I work as carefully as I can to stay with the language and with the concepts of the people we interview. I have come to believe that the language people use and the other practices they live and talk about are extremely important.

To reinterpret their language, to place it in alien "scientific concepts" is, I believe, a colonial activity. It is an imposition, an external invasion of the practices that constitute their very lives. Yet, as surely convinced as I am that I want to avoid such imperial activity, all the more certain I am that I will violate this principle myself. I think particularly of my use of words like control, protest, resistance, strategy, and tactics. These are not, as I use them, the language of the hard living. I employ them as "summaries" of practices which are well in evidence among the hard living. If I inadvertently use them without significant illustration of what they describe, I have been unfaithful to my intent.

My plan is to be as descriptive of the hard living and of the pastors and their churches as I can be given the character of our stories and conversations. I want to be as thickly descriptive of what we were told as I am able. Obviously the format of the book is mine, the frame of interpretation, and the selection of material is mine, but I have tried to write as plainly as possible using everyday language. As you read this book you should also watch out for those paragraphs when I move even more explicitly into an interpretive mode.

1

GROWING UP HARD
AND HOUSEHOLD RELATIONS

Margaret ran away from home at fourteen when her parents got divorced. By the time she was fifteen, she had hitchhiked, "three times around the United States." She was on her own throughout her teenage years. "I had a lot of fun experiences, different." During her early teen years she got an apartment in a large midwestern city. She wanted to be on her own "because I was seeing my friends and seeing the rut they was in and going through the same rut with them, and I just wanted a change, and I figured if I never got out of here, I'd never get out of that rut that they was in."

Margaret reports that she continued to go to school until the tenth grade, keeping her travels confined to summers, when "I just decided it was time to pick up and go . . . then it was fall, time for school to start. I'd always come back and gone to school and then like I said, I quit school in the tenth grade."

Asked what it was like to be fourteen and on her own she replies: "I don't know, it was different, I never really felt fourteen. I don't remember having much of a childhood, I guess, because of all my brothers and sisters I grew up so fast." She is the youngest of twelve children, and five of them are now deceased, having died at relatively young ages.

"My parents was away from home quite a bit, so I just grew up really fast. Fourteen wasn't anything to me," she reports as she then laughs to herself. "People who knew me then, and them being adult and me being a child, they say it was amazing that someone could live and support their self and do the things I did."

Margaret made her way by working as a dishwasher in restaurants and later as a laborer unloading semitrailer trucks. "I'd help unload trucks, and I'd make money there, and then a lot of them would offer to buy you dinner after unloading trucks with them, and so that's basically how you live."

She finally left school for good on Christmas Eve when she "packed up." "It was snowing, I was still watching my friends and myself in the same rut. At that time drugs was very popular, and I knew if I stayed here, I would continue doing what my friends done, and I would continue doing drugs with my friends, so I packed up and hitchhiked to Houston, Texas, which I spent close to four years. I got me a job down there."

The most difficult period of her life was the three years she spent separated from her parents when she was a child. A brother of hers was seriously ill, and she was sent to live with neighbors down the street. While she states that "they were very good to me," being without her family and not fully understanding why she was sent away were "one of the hardest times of my life." She knew that she was the only child not in school at the time, but, still she did not completely comprehend that when she was four and five years old.

Margaret's story is not unusual among hard living people. Tough struggles in the family, battles with poverty and near poverty, spending large amounts of childhood time on one's own, the experience of emotionally hard separations from parents through financial difficulties, divorce, death, sometimes just plain abandonment, independent living at a youthful age, heavy drug and alcohol use, hitchhiking around the country, pick-up jobs, and sometimes entanglements with the law or the courts: All these experiences appeared with an almost numbing regularity in the lives of the people with whom we talked.

Boyce, an African American born in Mississippi, was raised by his mother. "My father left when I was real young. I remember my Mom was pregnant at the time. There were seven kids. She had a baby boy, and I was only five years old. Dad came in drunk. He had spent all the money . . . Dad used to come in drunk and spend all the money and be hungry and stuff. Mom use to get on him . . . and they would be fighting. Then he would hit Mom. Then all of us would get hit and then he left. Then I didn't see him in about [trying to remember the last time]. I seen him at my sister's funeral, you know."

Ken's Dad was killed in World War II "someplace in Germany, I think. We was real hard up. We was lucky Mom had a job. She was never home. She got to going with a guy that hated us kids. We ended up spending most of our time at Grandpa's place in the country."

"My brother and sister were pretty good in school. They both got jobs after school. I hated school. Instead of going, I used to go to Grandpa's. He didn't care if I went to school or not. Mom didn't either. I guess I got to the sixth grade.

"I got a job with the section crew on the railroad when I was sixteen. I got to playing around with this gal and got her pregnant. She was sixteen or seventeen; I don't remember. I was seventeen. Her old man made us get married. I was gone all the time on the railroad construction crew. After the baby was born, we split up. She got married again I think. Haven't heard from her . . . can't remember the kid."

FATHERS AND MOTHERS

"My father . . . He wasn't never there for me." While Burton's father worked, "he wasn't taking care of home." He was working and doing something with his money. I don't know what he was doing. . . . I'll tell you something . . . I ain't never set down and talked with my father for thirty years. Never just set down, me and the man."

Marcel's mother married when she was fourteen and his

father was forty. "I was an accident. The rubber broke and here I am." When he first made the statement Marcel seemed to be making a joke of it, but then he detailed the shuffle back and forth between his parents and grandparents. His mother, and he with her, went through a series of marriages and divorces, "six or seven." When Marcel found out for the first time that he had been "an accident, it upset me very much."

Then, as he talked about how important it was for parents "to be straight up," his bitterness toward his mother became quite evident.

Rhonda's mamma died when she was three, but her father, a truck driver "who never drank or smoked" would take her on trips with him, one of the highlights of her life. Her father, three brothers, and she were a close-knit family, went to church and deeply loved each other. Then he died when Rhonda was in the tenth grade, and all the children had to go out on their own. Rhonda and two brothers went to work with a concessions outfit that traveled with a rodeo. Later, when she wanted a nine-to-five job, she found herself ill-prepared by her rodeo experience. During a series of hard times she wound up in Wichita without a place to stay and with no money to get back home to Kansas City. She brightened in the conversation when she remembered that "Daddy never switched me except one time when I didn't do my chores. We were both in tears."

ABUSE

Ross never knew his "real father." He says he had "eight stepfathers," who were everything from chief detectives to drug dealers. He had "constant fights" with them. "Two of my stepfathers put me in the hospital approximately seven times a piece. It wasn't a very good childhood, you might say." After moving out of the house when he was twelve years old, Ross explains that "the only reason was because his mother was an alcoholic. I was putting her to bed . . . I couldn't deal with it.

Started smoking dope when I was eight, started drinking when I was fourteen. You know, it's been an interesting life."

While there are exceptions to a history of abuse, as in the case of Rhonda above, it nevertheless enters the stories of most hard living people again and again. Charlotte was molested by one of her mother's brothers-in-law, but was "told to keep quiet about it." Jo Ann's mother was an alcoholic and prostitute who would pass out after doing a trick. Some of these men would then come to Jo Ann's room. This happened from the time she was fourteen until she ran away from home two years later. Carol was raped at age twelve. One woman was raped immediately after her husband's funeral by "a friend" who had come over to comfort her.

Such sexual abuse occurred with men as well, though not nearly as frequently, as in the case of Earl and his mother. "One day my mother asked me if I have ever had sex with any woman. I told her 'No.' Then she said, 'It's good for a mother to show her son how to have sex.' So I had sex with my mother several times. But we broke off when I started stealing from her for drugs." Another man, Jerry, told us that his drunken father had tried to rape him when he was thirteen. Drinking and family instability were "part of my life story. I have suffered from depression all my life."

To hear stories like these and to realize how much the hard living are demeaned in a world populated with indignities, in a world that regards them as "trash," is to get in touch with enormous pain. To know that so much of one's life is out of control, to have the tracks of failure all around, to experience life as not responsive to your will and aims, and yet to be told that you are at fault, to want so much the love of family and to endure an abusive violation of self that bespeaks a worthlessness of the most fundamental kind, or sometimes, to know the love of mother and father only to have them ripped away in death, to find life so rut-filled and violence-prone that one cannot stay put even when there is no place to go: These are the things of which hard living is made.

Women and Men

Country music runs a gamut from "Heartbreak Hotel" to "Nobody knows what goes on behind closed doors," from "Cold, Cold Heart" to "I'm in love again." Blues, jazz, rap, and just about *any* form of music that is tied to men and women (and especially to those who are poor or near-poor) will convey the struggle with their relationships. The lives of the hard living vibrate with these same struggles. One finds the battle between the sexes, but one also discovers people who seem to love each other deeply; one finds breakup, but also love. As the stories explain, abuse, violence, and exploitation of women also characterize many of these relationships, but there are as well those who say they could not make it without the man or woman in their lives.

People like Mack have been married only once and for a long time. Mack's spouse earns the family income; he has health problems. While they have had a "rough time" financially, their relationship seems secure and strong. In fact, when asked about their marriage, their biggest issue, except for their budgetary problems, seems to be his "language," which his wife describes as "naughty naughties." Mack says his speech gets worse when he hangs around "a certain character" too much. He wants to go back to work, but his wife protests: "No, you ain't. You fought [his health problems] this long for it, so keep fighting."

Beatrice, too, has been married virtually all her adult life, but her husband has ongoing problems with depression, work-related injuries, and, for a time, alcohol. "When he was drinking, he would yell at me. Weekends were the worst. Eventually he got professional help and has been dry for ten years." Beatrice is one of those people who does not complain although she has had "a hard life" according to those who know her, and we shall get to know her better later, but her husband says that she has "ice in her veins" because she rarely gets rattled.

One wonders, of course, what price the women in both these marriages have paid in order to keep family and children together. Their struggle for order against the chaotic invasions of illness, drink, and hardship, even the effort to keep certain language out of their lives bespeaks the unending, laborious, necessity-bound endeavor required to stay just beyond disaster.

The overwhelming majority of the people we interview were married or had live-in relationships, more than once. Some had been wed six or seven times, and others had moved from one live-in to another throughout most of their adult lives.

Cheryl got divorced after fifteen years of marriage to a man who beat her and once tried to stab her, but she now is engaged to someone she describes as "a good man" who "needs her." She points out how "tenderhearted he is," how he needs her "to listen to and be with him." Making it quite clear that they are not live-ins, but only spend time together, she speaks warmly of how "he stuck by me" when a brother and a friend both died of cancer within a short time of each other about a year ago. "Now it's my turn to stick by him."

Alton and Jo Ann lived together for about a year and a half, each of them having had other relationships in the past. Alton, an African American, found Jo Ann, white, "on the streets, doing drugs, turning tricks, stealing, and doing all kinds of things in order to support herself." Reporting that she was "stuck on crack" and that her addiction caused her much difficulty, Alton invited her to move into his small, barely furnished apartment in an effort to help. Jo Ann was asked how long she had been doing drugs. Having been quiet and subdued up to this point she jumps in to clarify things, and she says to Alton with some feeling: "Don't say a damned thing because I'm not the only one that uses." She clearly implies that Alton as a user is in no position to judge her need for drugs.

As both then open up, Jo Ann said that she met and immediately liked Alton "because he was 'bad' and without a doubt, he wouldn't take no shit off nobody." Alton, in turn, explains—that he is not a junkie like Jo Ann, but only "a casual user." He seems quite protective of her and said that he "had been exposed to how a man should take care of his woman." His hope is "to land a decent job which would be steady" so that he could at least find "a decent place for us to live." Jo Ann wants to get married, but Alton states that "I don't need no paper to tell me who my woman is." He feels that "the fact that I am with her says that."

Bob had been married and the father of three children. He had a good job that paid well, but his wife split: "She took off with a black guy, some nigger she met at work. That didn't last long. She come back, but I divorced her anyway." He plunged into this report of his previous marriage and divorce after being asked about his life since his time in the military. The comment above is, by the way, one of the very few racist remarks or racial slurs in all of the interviews we conducted.

"Well, she got a better lawyer than I had. She ended up getting the kids. She said I was an unfit father. I guess I did stop off on the way home. I did party a bit, and I did spend some money on cars and trucks. She got a job and had money for her and the kids. Anyway, the judge really put the screws on me. I ended up with about seventy-five bucks a week to live on. I had to get a part-time job for a little while."

"I turned in some work simp.[simplification] ideas and made a pile here [at an assembly plant], but she got some of that too. I almost got a gun and shot her a couple times. I took that work simp. money and paid off my place. She didn't want that. I almost quit this place, too. I couldn't see working this hard for her getting seventy-five percent. She got remarried to some guy, and she is still tying up my paycheck about once a month. She drags my ass into court about twice a year over everything you can think of. Every time I get a raise, she finds out about it and comes to get her share for the kids. These last five years have been pure hell, I want to tell you. All because I'm just a hardworking man who needs a little fun once in a while."

Bob has since remarried. "She takes care of me. If I party, it is at our house, and she's there. She's got a good job, but *we* come first!"

Early marriage leads to divorce for many of those we interview. Roy reports about his divorce after fifteen years of marriage: "I got married a day after my eighteenth birthday . . . I think the biggest thing was that we were kids when we got married, and then we grew up. She had different interests than I did." His daughter had said a few months ago: "Dad, I never did see you and Mom argue." Roy goes on, "It's a tough world any more being a kid. When I was a kid, you might of heard of someone being divorced, but now days being divorced is just like buying a new car. A guy shouldn't make little of it. It is a shame. It's too fast a world any more."

Anna's experience is more turbulent. She worked as a prostitute for a couple of years, but did not want to talk much about it. All she would say was that she had "a top notch pimp" who did not beat her and who had helped her out several times since she had gotten out of the business. After leaving prostitution she immediately married a man who was an alcoholic. Although it was not a good marriage, she did soon have two children, and they made the situation tolerable. She eventually lost custody of them, however, to her father and stepmother. Seeing them only occasionally she nevertheless speaks quite proudly of the children. After a divorce, she spent the next few years "playing" and wound up getting into "a lot of trouble," upon which she did not elaborate. When she married again, it was to a cocaine addict from whom she is now separated and plans to divorce as soon as she can get together enough money.

The range of relationships between women and men is enormous among the hard living. Mack and the husband of Beatrice are semi-invalids and depend on their wives for the family income. If Beatrice seems more stoic and ready to face a tough world with ice water in her veins, Mack's wife encourages him not to go back to work but gets nettled with his "naughty" language. Yet, both of these women face a future where neither can foresee an end to the struggle they now live out. Cheryl has found a man whose loyalty makes her want to stick by him. Alton sees himself as the protector of Jo Ann, albeit one that is paternalistic and not prepared to ratify the relationship through marriage, a hedge not shared by Jo Ann. More than that, his resistance to marriage seems to leave most of the choices up to him. Their poverty and their meagre existence do not, moreover, bode well for the future. Bob's male social needs got him into even deeper financial difficulty when his first marriage ended, and his former spouse seems to be extraordinarily sagacious in knowing how to exact child support from him, a process that has not endeared Bob to her nor encouraged any altruistic spirit toward his children. It has, however, transformed his second marriage, at least according to his report. Some, like Ray, marry too early, and others, like Anna, find their primary relationships and husbands while doing the dangerous work of prostitution. These stories, however, only illustrate something of the relationships that men and women hold. They do not by any means display the range of these among the hard living. If anything characterizes their lives together, it would be that all of the relationships are hard in terms of money, living space, drugs, health, or something. None of the relationships is easy.

CHILDREN

The hard living grow up to be parents and sometimes take their children through a repeat performance of their same experience. Elliot lives on the streets and ekes out an existence through a variety of hustles and coping skills. He has been separated from his children for some time, but when he begins to talk about what he wants for the future, his children surface immediately. "I got five children. When I get settled down, I'm going to get them. I want them to have what I never had, love and care, things I never had. I am there for that. They know where I am at, they know I'm down here. They can call me and

I'll be right there. I feel there is a piece of me in each one of them. One is quiet, one is mean, and one is evil and likes to get into trouble." Elliot's hopes for his children are straight forward: "Stay away from drugs, stay in school, get a good life. Don't worry about Dad, I'll be here for you. If your life needs to move on, go ahead; don't wait on nobody." Elliot, who spent ten years in the penitentiary on murder convictions, has been out seven years and was living in a homeless shelter when we talked to him.

Dawn "went to school" on the treatment she received from her parents. When she and her sister told their grandmother that their father was sleeping with them and molesting them, they were taken in by family services, and Dawn grew up in four different foster homes. "When you grow up in foster homes, you get a secure life, but it's not the same as having your mom and dad there when you cry or you get sick and have them by your side. Those things I missed out on . . . I hate my mom for it . . . you know I don't . . . I think she had a hard life, too, trying to raise six kids by herself. But she had it rough . . . I sometimes still don't understand why she didn't try to get us back, you know, sooner. That's one question she never answered [before she died]. That really bothers me."

Now as the mother of four children herself Dawn intends for their lives to be very different. For a time she struggled with alcoholism and stopped drinking when she realized how much she was hurting her children and her husband. She is now determined not to be like her mother. "I feel my mom gave up on me . . . That would be the last thing I would *ever* do to my own. I want them to know that they can come and talk to me about anything, and I'll be there, if it is right or wrong. My mom never did that kind of stuff. 'Well [acting like her mother] you play, you lay in it; you make your bed, you lay in it.' It was never, 'well, I'll be by your side if you need me!' " Now deeply committed to her children and her husband, Dawn seems to be ready and able to make her commitments stick.

With others the contradictions are much more present. "On her own" since she was seventeen years old Lavonna, now twenty-eight, claims she has been "a hooker" since she was fourteen. Her first child's father had promised to marry her "but lied and ran off." This child is "a crack baby" she says, and she has "tried to get cleaned up" since she discovered she was pregnant again. She confessed that she has not been very successful and admits to using coke several times during this pregnancy. Lavonna knows, of course, that her life-style is hazardous for her and the children, but she has "to do something to support the family." While she is on public assistance, her check is too little compared to her bills for food, rent, utilities, and everything else. She assured the interviewer, however, that she "never puts my kids in danger" because she always goes well-away from her place to turn tricks. "I would never allow any 'john' to know where I live." When asked about her greatest fear for her children, she replied: "That my children would grow up in the projects and not really get a chance in life." "Project dwellers," as she called herself, "were in many cases, not given a chance to prove themselves because of where they came from."

In these interviews I am struck with the contradictions, and I do not mean this in a judgmental way. Rather I mean it in the sense that our culture prescribes norms and ideals which seem to be deeply stained in the minds of the hard living. Yet, the very structure of their lives—in most cases, from the time they are born—so defies these ideals. Elliot wants to "be there" for his children, but he is eight hundred miles away from them, impoverished, living in a homeless shelter, a convicted murderer who has done time, who is hooked on drugs, and hustles the street to survive. Dawn seems like a fine mother and a loving companion to her husband. She learned her parenting from the bad example of her sexually abusive father and a mother who "never tried to get us back." Dawn is, by all that we could see, a lover and a provider of nurture, but how much permanent damage remains from her father's abuse? Her slip of the tongue in which she says she hates her mother is probably true, but that she also loves her is not a strange conflict, perhaps, for most people, but with her history it must take on a special poignancy and disturbance. Lavonna already has one crack baby and is doubtlessly now carrying another. She testifies that she "never puts her kids in danger" from her tricks, but the one born and the one coming have already been imperiled by her drug use, a jeopardy even more predictable than exposure to her "johns," as hazardous as that clearly is.

Hearing these stories I find myself in a rage against Elliot's father who left him to the streets, or Dawn's who violated her and her mother who did not stand up to him, or Lavonna's husband who "ran off," or her parents. But, then, every time I trace back a tragedy in one generation I find another in the generation before. One cannot help but wonder what testimony of poverty and sheer hell I would hear from Elliot's father, or who, probably, abused Dawn's father in the home where he was raised, or what desert of neglect or storm of fury devastated the parents of Lavonna. In such searches the realization comes that no help can be found from looking to the past for blame. The only hope comes in a future which can be changed.

As detrimental to such change and as large an obstacle as any is that of drug abuse. Perhaps nothing looms with so much foreboding on the everyday lives of the hard living.

2

THE DRUG WORLD AND THE REAL WORLD

I can control everything, anything . . . you know, I ain't gonna let drugs control my life, I told myself, and at that time I didn't realize [the power drugs had over me] . . . I was spending all the money turning everybody on, but they was beating me at the same time. I'd cash in dope, and the dope dealer told me to go buy my own pipe and learn to torch it myself. With that he gave me a half a gram on credit. I paid it back the next day . . . I mastered it real well. I had people delivering it to my job. I was cool. [Then,] I really got strung out, but I didn't think I had a problem. And I noticed I started waking up late, sleeping over, not wanting to go to work, borrowing a whole lot of money from my boss, and I did a whole lot of stealing. I got to doing things that I thought I'd never do. I mean, I started stealing, selling everything that was mine and others, or pawning it, or trading it . . . I was a good person, I really was. People depended on me . . . but now that I got into drugs . . . my life just turned completely around."

Jack *was* a good person and a mechanic, a fine one. He could always get work that paid well. He had plenty of money. He helped out friends and family until he entered the drug world.

It is a world, a cosmos unto itself, a completely engrossing reality with its own rules and "normality," its canons of status and sources of power. For many it is the only world they know. Reports of blackouts that last for days, even weeks, distort memories so that people talk about months, even years, in their lives that they cannot recall anything except for flashes of pictures triggered by the events of a day but displayed more like a collage of moments pieced together out of a lost past. It is a violent world, a place of beatings and rapes, of knives and gunshot wounds, of quick lethal conflicts, of overdose, and of that long slow slide into the complicated health problems of repeated drug abuse. It is a world with its own moralities of evil serving the incessant and unquenchable *telos* of the fix. No kinship, no friendship bonds as deeply as the screaming hunger for a chemical peace.

The entrances into this world are many. Agnes began with marijuana when she was eight years old. "By the time I was eleven I was an out of control kid; I was running amuck. When I was fourteen my mother had me removed from the house." Sam reported: "all my life I have been drinking. It began when I was twelve. I drank through school. I joined the army and continually drank in the service. I became uncontrollable when I was twenty-two." Ross smoked pot at eight years of age, drank at eleven, and was selling and using hard drugs by the time he was twenty-two. His drug abuse and drug dealing landed him in the penitentiary for five years. When he was released and walked out the gate, "I was scared, the only thing I knew how to do was to deal drugs," in spite of the fact that he had learned several skilled trades while he was locked up.

Kitty complains that she got in with the wrong crowd. Joe says his troubles began the night of the senior prom when he decided to get drunk instead of going to the dance. A number of people talked about things like unbelievably bad times, the death of a child or close family member, an avalanche of bills, divorce, an uncontrollable anger, a decision to get even with someone, rebellion against one's parents, a way to be "cool," and on and on. For so many the drug abuse in its compulsive fury seems genetic, at least at base, like some terror-by-night disease and/or some tragic, allergic reaction that lasts a lifetime and ravages everyone known to the victim.

Why? What causes this dictatorial, totalitarian control over one's life, a control so powerful it turns all waking moments into an unbroken subservience to a reign of slavery and finally, if not overthrown, of death. The answers to this question are probably not finally known and may not be ultimately knowable. Todd speaks as powerfully to the cause of drug abuse as anyone: "A normal person doesn't know how he's gonna feel the next minute. A drunk does. He just can't stand reality. With dope you know how you're going to feel. It is a world where money and drugs mean everything."

As Burton says, "on the streets drugs and money are power. You can get just about anything, you know. Drugs kinda bring the money. If you got drugs, you'll get money. If you keep drugs, you get respect. You can get rich in a month's time." Burton's problems began, however, "when I became my best customer." When that happened, he lost the money, the power, and the respect. "When the money is gone and the crack is gone, everybody is gone. You haven't got no power no more. Everybody splits when you got no money, no drug power."

This is a world of victims, victims who are victimized by yet other victims. Joan has a history of mental illness, of deep depressions for which she has been hospitalized a number of times and returns to a psychiatric clinic even now as a woman in her late forties. Her story was told so matter-of-fact that I had to keep reminding myself of the reality of what she was saying. She admits of becoming "a little wild" in her thinking which led her to begin visiting bars, a "spree" that resulted from her loneliness and lack of friends. Then within the same ten minutes of conversation she reports three rapes, including a gang rape. While it is true that some of what she says is simply too unreal to believe, the detail—this strange commentary about horrendous occurrences that she reports like an external observer of some sterile clinical event—is so concrete and so specific that it must be true. She has had a child out of wedlock, an attempted suicide, two divorces, another stay in a psychiatric hospital, repeated robberies, and suffers recurring cycles of depression. No wonder.

What is perhaps most strange of all about the drug world is how real and normal it seems to those caught in its bondage. Agnes speaks of selling drugs in her teens and twenties and "thought it was normal." As we learned above, Agnes had been doing drugs since she was eight, was running "amuck" at eleven, and "removed" from her home at fourteen. She then went into a group home for several months, which she "didn't like," and from there "went into a marriage based on drugs, hoping this would pull me out from under my mother's eye." Over the course of this marriage Agnes had two children, but the relationship with her husband turned out to be extremely abusive. Still, "we sold drugs, and I thought it was normal. I really didn't think it was okay to steal, to buy drugs, but then I began to do it. I think I lost touch with my conscience through drugs and alcohol. When the marriage ended, I started drinking even more."

Agnes tells the story in which she and her live-in went to a friend's house who was dealing. They were sitting in the living room when two men broke through the door and shot the friend.

While her partner took the drugs out of the house to hide them from the impending police investigation, the wounded man's small son kept asking her over and over and over again, "Why did they shoot my dad?" Agnes kept answering "Because they are bad people." Agnes then commented, "But they were doing what we did. It just all seemed so normal."

Todd also talked about the reality and the normality of the drug world. "The system we lived in was not real, it was created by us. Heavy drug use rules; it becomes so fucking real. It becomes normal. For years I didn't go to bed without a fix on the chest of drawers for when I woke up. Your whole life is built around drugs."

Once going to "a normal house" Todd recounts sitting there

and repeatedly saying to himself, "This is real; what I'm doing isn't. This is real; what I'm doing isn't. This is real; what I'm doing isn't." One can readily see why the drug world and a steady job are such contradictions.

WORK

Most of the hard living people have uneven employment from their teenage years. In large part this grew out of the poverty, the limited education, and the constrained opportunities they faced. The relationship of these factors to drug abuse which, of course, powerfully affected their work records is difficult to assess in terms of which was more important except to say that the impact of poverty and drug abuse together was in each case devastating.

Many report a string of various jobs "connected" by periods of unemployment. Ross had been a cab driver, mowed lawns, worked in a low-paying factory, sold concessions at a stadium, and had been a maintenance man, but he said he "only mainly knew one thing, how to do and sell drugs." Yet, when we talked with him, he had been drug free for some time, had a new job in maintenance, and was on his way with his live-in to begin this work the next day.

Some picked up a variety of skills like tending bar, barbering, hairdressing, food service, and so on, but drug abuse kept these jobs brief and sporadic. Others did temporary work, meeting early in the morning at job depots to be handpicked by employers for single day jobs. Jimmy says of these: "you got to be willing to work, and they [the unemployed] don't want to work. They're just a bunch of winos, and that's all there is to it." Talcott reported that he had "done just about every kind of job possible," but all of his jobs were handyman type work. Never having the opportunity to get any schooling and having been raised in a poor farm family with ten children in Oklahoma, he had to help his father with the work. He finally left the farm "to find my fortune in the city."

Finding a good job isn't easy. One man says that the employers won't look at people who have had a hard time. "If someone has quit school, there's a bunch of them places that won't even look at 'em. Unless you've got a GED or a high school diploma, larger companies won't even attempt to look at somebody for employment."

Of course, a good many of the hard living at some time in their lives make it by hustling. Some of them do it throughout their adult years. Jimmy told us "I could make my living with a stick [shooting pool], so I didn't really need a job at the time." He reported that when he tended bar, they would close the place at 3 a.m. and then "we'd shut the doors . . . and shoot until six in the morning. We'd make $300 to $500 a game . . . I could walk out of a bar with $200 a night." Most of the hustling, however, takes place around buying and selling drugs. The problem with this, though, is holding onto the money. The hard living people we talked with almost to a person use their earnings to consume the very products they sell.

Occasionally we got insights into what "good jobs" were. It is often painful just to see how little they want. Carol is speaking proudly of her new position. "Here I am in raggedy blue jeans, cut-off sweatshirt, answering phones, having people fill out applications for apartments, and showing apartments. I am the assistant manager trainee . . . My boss is very picky. He just handed me the keys to the office today. I can come in and run things. I can come and go as I want. Just lock it up and put my sign in the window, Manager Out for a Minute.' Go show my apartment and come and go as I want. I got the run of the place. I got control of all the keys. I don't have to dress up for this job. The boss takes me at face value. He knows I can work. Don't have to look . . . " she paused, almost as if she did not want to talk about her clothing or lack of it. "That has always been my problem cause I don't have the money to dress. Most office jobs you have to look so-so. It is too much bother to me really. I don't care if my Gucci bag matches my alligator shoes. I don't wear a bouffant." She then laughs at her self-parody.

Jack's dream is to have his own shop. "There's good money [in car repair], 'cause I worked with a friend. I ran his shop. We made good money. A lot of people I knew—people I grew up with, even the guys I worked with—they would tell me: 'you gonna be all right, you gonna make it!' They wanted me to open up my own shop. I was headed that way . . . until I got headed into the wrong turn." He explains: "I started smoking that coke. I lost everything, . . . but there's a lot of things out there that I'd like to see and do. And I will. I mean, you know, not tomorrow, but I will. In time." Most of the hard living, however, do not have much hope in terms of concrete job expectations. They often express dreams of a home, a car, the family being together, and a good job. Yet, for most, this seems like a distant if not impossible dream.

WINNERS

Six of the people we interviewed, however, are what I call hard living winners. They are members of a union, work on an assembly line, and have high wages and good benefits. Yet all of them have histories of violence, unstable households, heavy alcohol/drug use , and, until they got on the assembly line, irregular employment.

Without exception these half dozen hard living winners, while not uncritical, are clear in their support of the union. They know that it not only guarantees good wages and benefits but job security as well. Gene speaks for them all when he says: "Well I can't believe that all people don't have unions. There's no other way that they are going to get ahead than through a union. The lowest jobs are nonunion jobs."

Ken also speaks with appreciation for the union, "I wouldn't work anywhere without a union. I joined right away when I worked for the railroad. I joined right away here [at the assembly plant]. You can't trust foremen. It takes the union to keep them honest. The union has helped me a lot."

But they can also be quite critical. Bob was still upset because of the reaction of the union to his work simplification ideas for which he received additional cash compensation: "I have paid a dear price [for the work simplification programs]. The union guys are on my ass. I lost some good friends. They call me 'suck-ass' and other kinds of things. I even dropped out of the union for a while." It has, however, "kind of blown over."

Gibson is critical of unions because of the entrance of women into jobs traditionally held for men. He says about the unions: "they do their best. It's a different world. They spend their time helping women who can't do their jobs. The factory is no place for a woman. They know nothing about mechanical things. We all have to help them. They don't want to work overtime; yet they cheat to make as much as they can on piecework." He believes that women should "absolutely not" work in a factory. "My ole lady is never coming here to work if I can help it."

Gibson also thinks that unions are "not as good as they used to be. Too many guys think only about themselves. They don't stick together. It's every man for himself kinda. It didn't used to be that way. We looked out for each other."

Yet, if they can be critical of the union, they can be deeply hostile and disparaging of management, especially young men fresh out of college. Gibson says: "Management is trying to break the union. The last two contracts we went on strike for no reason, except the company wanted us out of here because they had too much inventory in the field. You just can't trust these college boy managers. They lie; they try to cheat you . . . they never did a day's work in their lives, and they should be paying the company to work here, no more than they do."

Similar feelings are expressed by Bob. "There are so many things we could do for the company, if they would just listen. Those young college boys are stupid. All it takes is a little common sense, and we could save them a lot of money. I like to work on new ideas, but the engineers don't think I know anything. The guy in the shop is a lot smarter. The company and the union keep arguing about how we should work to make things better. They are just protecting their turf. The guys in the shop will end up paying for both sides' stupidity."

This theme of getting credit for "knowing something" occurs steadily with the hard living winners. Gene virtually summarizes his work life around the issue: "I started in a know-nothing, do-nothing job. I now run a machine. I've gained a lot of knowledge."

Roy is frustrated because he feels that the company is not interested in his ideas. More than that, he likes a job that had a diversity of things to do. He wants some changes but sees little chance of it. "To me, if I do something different every day, it makes a perfect day. But my machine's sat here in the same corner for twelve years. I didn't mind my work, but there was no challenge anymore. I don't expect to run the place some day, but it would be nice to be recognized for the few brains you do have."

Still, the most important part of hard living winners' lives is not what happens on the job but away from it. Gibson mentioned hunting and fishing. Our interviewer said in response: "You mentioned fishing and hunting as a hobby." Gibson corrected him immediately, "It's not a hobby. It's what I do outside my work. I live on the river in the woods. I'm my own boss out there. Even the law doesn't come out there. I can drink as much as I want and do what I please after I leave this place. My family loves it. My boys are good woodsmen. It's hard to keep them going to school."

Fitting In

"I have always been in the back seat of the family." This is the way Mack describes his experience. He also says he was "the dark sheep. It always seemed like when I was growing up, even today when I am around them, I say I am different.

They always seem to be talking down to me, as if to say: 'What are you doing here?' or words to that effect. The way they look at me." According to Mack his own family seems to act as if they are superior to him. He tells one painful story about his brother coming to town. "When my youngest brother was in town oh, it has been a year, year and a half ago—with his son . . . He came to town to fix up his wife's house, and I wanted to get together with him. They say 'no' cause I made him too damn nervous." When asked why, Mack says, "Beats the hell out of me, and I hadn't seen him in . . . two or three years. Maybe its because of our ages, I don't know. But you see, whenever I am around my family, I feel out of place." Later, he adds that "My family has never treated me like I was one of them. In other words, they told me to go stand off in a dunce's corner, which I suppose I have done most of my life instead of standing up and telling them occasionally to go straight to hell. . . ."

Mack's story, while different in details, is quite common among the hard living in terms of feeling out of place, of not quite "connecting" with people or even with the world. In the same conversation reported immediately above, Mack said that he felt most like himself when he was alone.

Joan, when she was growing up, "felt like the dumbest one of the bunch." She has wanted friends all her life, just "someone to talk to," but she "felt like an outcast." She claims that "I never had anybody of my own." Remembering her high school days, when classmates were having dates and holding down jobs, she says that "I got the feeling I wasn't anything."

Larry was raised partly "in an orphanage home" and partly by his father's parents. His mother left him and his father when he was a child. Larry had only seen her again about six months before. This reunion left him with a very painful sense of abandonment. She had "gotten involved with another man and has three more kids." When Les was twelve his father was killed in a car crash. He admitted to having a chip on his shoulder because he lost his dad and didn't know his mother.

His stepmother now lives in Baton Rouge. Larry sums up his experience with the comment that "Everybody's trying to find love," but then he says, "you don't get to touch anything in this world."

Others felt disconnected from people and circumstances, but this took other forms. If Mack and Joan and Larry can speak longingly for what might have been, others take a more defiant stance. Todd says that "I didn't fit in. The only notoriety I could get was to act out. In our family you weren't supposed to get angry. So when I did, it was rage, and rage is contagious and dangerous, and it escalates." This rage, as Todd sees it, was a basic reason for his spending twelve years in prison before he was thirty-five years old.

Some felt pressure to fit in, to make it, and yet experienced the pressure itself as debilitating. Jack remembers that his dad would "always tell me I know you are gonna be something,' you know, and I didn't realize it at the time, but . . . that started putting a lot of pressure on me. Everybody's expecting me to do this and be that. I wish they weren't." Jack also recalls that "when I was drugging and using, he would throw that in my face all the time, 'Boy, I knew you was gonna be something . . . You sure let me down.' And he was right, I let myself down, like I said, I should have been married. I mean when I was out of school. I had a wonderful lady. And I broke her heart. And I been thinking about it to this day, you know. I should have been married and had two cars, *two* . . . the house, the dog, you know . . . I blew it all, it all went up in smoke, as they say."

Talcott blames himself. "My biggest problem is myself." He reports that he never "really opened up to many people," and his friends were limited to "just a few bums who hung around down at the Salvation Army." He seems to accept his circumstances without blaming anyone or anything else except himself.

With Eric we get bravado. He speaks of his strong "self-esteem" and that "only the strong can be down and get back." He speaks of a past time in his life when he woke up with a bed full of hundred dollar bills. He once owned fancy cars and big houses. Now having a "permanent woman," whom he has not married, he has two children with her. He sees himself as a "hustler," but she is "fed up." Hers is a lonely life, as Eric sees it. She is "a Christian woman." Eric, however, is "international" because he has a woman in each of four cities. On several occasions during the interview he declared vehemently, "I'm real. I be myself."

With most of the hard living there is a sense of the reality of their own lives as something to be protected. They experience the expectations of others, of society as encroachment, as a kind of aggression against who they are. For some, like Todd above, their reaction is defiant and hostile, but most, who may not be as explosive as Todd, nevertheless are resistant to the notion of being turned into something they are not. Lana, for example, was actually raised in an affluent home, one where she was "protected" and "could do no wrong." By her own report she was not disciplined, had everything she wanted, and was sheltered. At the same time high expectations came with this treatment. "I was supposed to be the perfect person. I didn't want to be perfect. I wasn't perfect. If I skipped school, my mother would believe that they made a mistake in the school records because her daughter wouldn't do that. Excuses were made for me. And they tried to make me into something I wasn't."

Lana has three children, but they have not lived with her now for some time. "I don't do well with kids," she says. "I should have never had them. I am not real motherly. I thought it was my duty. So I did what everyone expects me to do, again."

She likes the homeless shelter where she is now. It is a family environment without the expectations of sexual intimacy that she has found previously with her husbands and other men. "I had a tendency to get in with men in my past. I didn't care if I loved them, but it was someone to come home to. Here I have my own room. If I want company, it is here without any sexual, intimate expectation. We can just go talk to someone."

Lana is also clear that she wants to continue to work at the shelter and not move back into mainstream society. "Who says that everyone needs a normal society living. Some people maybe can't deal with it. That doesn't make them bad; they can still function. They are kind of like in between a mental hospital [and the world outside]. I am not saying I am crazy, but there is a problem there . . . where they just wasn't made for the world out there. They have to deal with the world in a small area. Well, I can stay in this building. I can go to school and get a degree. What says I can't stay in a small world. Maybe a lot of people could deal a lot better if they had an environment that was smaller."

"It is like old people when they get old; they are better off in a nursing home. Now some hate it, but some really enjoy it. They have their friends they can talk to. They can play bingo. At their house there was never anyone that came by. There was never anyone that cared. They was forgotten. You know, it is kind of like here. Maybe I am a little girl that never grew up. Maybe I need that. There are counselors that are like a mother or father image that gave me advice, support when I did well, be there for me when I have a problem. I know when you grow up, you are supposed to take care of yourself. That is what is expected of you."

When I examine the interviews about people who felt so alien and unrelated to the world, I become suspicious. I accuse myself subjectively of choosing only the worst cases. The people discussed above, however, are not atypical but representative of those with whom we talked. I experience myself getting deeply depressed as I tried to imagine what it felt like to say and to believe the things they report about themselves. What is it like to be Mack, to be in one's late forties, to feel like the "back seat" of the family, to be "out of place," "a dunce," and to be most like oneself when alone? And to feel that way all of one's life? Or to be Joan and to see oneself as the "dumbest," "the outcast," who mainly "wanted friends to talk to"? Then her crushing comment, "I wasn't anything." It is, then, really not hard to understand Todd's rage and his attempt to get notoriety because he didn't fit in.

Even Eric's bombastic pretensions take on pathos. When he struts and claims "I'm real, I be myself," it seems strangely cruel to judge and dismiss him. It is like blaming a twisted and struggling tree in a dense forest for looking so queer while striving for the light. No wonder his "permanent woman" is "fed up," and one may ask why she does not leave this blustering lout? The answer is easy: because there is no place else to go. But what about his being "international" with "a woman in each of four cities"? I find myself wondering how he does "feel like a man" with the smell of failure all around him and a deepening inability to face her. What better way to escape the condemnation of her being fed up than to prove that one is still an "international" male? A man who hustles for a living, whose absences she must understand all too well?

The self-condemnation is no better. Talcott sees himself as his own worst problem, and Jack confesses that he "blew it all" and was not able to face the pressure. "It all went up in smoke." Lana has concluded that she was not made for the world out there, and that she does not need, really cannot cope with, life outside the shelter. She does finally wonder if she is a little girl who never grew up. I felt that she had long since arraigned, tried, and convicted herself on a charge that would require incarceration, albeit in the shelter, from "the world out there."

When it comes to hard living, perhaps Larry really says it, "you don't get to touch anything in this world." If so, Lana understands it quite well: "Some people just wasn't made for the world out there."

These self-assessments, these feelings, these expressions of indignity are profoundly connected to hard living experience with the church and their attitudes toward one of the pivotal institutions in society.

3

THE CHURCH

Just because you don't worship down on the corner, it doesn't mean you don't believe. God has brought me home many times when I couldn't have made it on my own," Ralph argues as he prepares to speak his mind about the church. He continues, "if the church would stop putting people down—you know, I am no good—you know I don't go to church, but I used to. We was both raised in the Methodist Church."

"Yeah," his brother Kerry chimes in, "and I would knock that preacher's teeth out right now!"

"That's beside the point, Kerry. What I am saying is, if they would start coming down to our level, looking at what we've got to look at, not what's been happening in the past but what's coming up. I went to church for a while over in Sedalia. They had everybody believing why try to make anything, cause what's the use if it's the end of the world."

"It *is* near by," Kerry offers.

"It may be, it might be next week, but it might be next century. They have people believing if you give to the church, the church will give to you. That's physical, a physical thing. You have to ask for help, and it has to be from God. God's the one who does this."

This brief piece of a conversation captures some very basic attitudes about the church among hard living people. There is little question of an intense hostility toward the church and its clergy, although the reasons vary, as we shall see. And, yet, almost to a person, one hears abiding testimony about God and divine providence in a world that runs pillar to post between disaster and survival.

It would be misleading, however, to suggest that all hard living people have negative views of the church. Quite a few have very positive attitudes. I want to look, then, at the way hard living people talk about the church, and why so many have such little use for it, and others had so much appreciation. In the next chapter we shall move on to their understandings of God.

HYPOCRITES

I am not surprised at the charge that "the church is full of a bunch of hypocrites." Anyone who has been around very many people very long has heard the criticism. With hard living people it is no different.

Alton, offers that "everyday he had seen people who lead a hypocritical life." He *does* say that the church is a "good place for people who are serious about making a commitment to the man upstairs."

Jo Ann says that she had no association of any kind with the church. So she doesn't have much bad to say, but she does think "church-folks were stuck up" and that she would be "out of place." The church cannot help her, she believes, because she was "not one of the poor people who would be desirable." When asked what makes a desirable poor person, she answers that it is "those persons who would kiss ass in order to get handouts or whatever." This, she said, she "would not do."

Such comments are typical. One does not have to go far at all to hear them.

What does surprise me is the responses of those who will not go to church because it would be an exercise in hypocrisy for *them* to do so. Marcel, a twenty-nine year old, recalls the time when he attended church as a boy. As he reached puberty, the girls began "to turn me on." Because he didn't want to be a hypocrite, he left the church. While he continues to care about the Bible and enjoyed conversations with his grandmother about it, and, while he reads Edgar Cayce and, again, talks with his grandmother about "what was going on in the world," he left the church because he doesn't "want to be one of those people who go to church on Sunday and to hell on Monday."

Alton, again, thought that the church is a good place for those "on that end," meaning people who were religiously inclined, but he is clear he would "never go to church" because he didn't "intend to be hypocritical."

Finally, John, reporting, a long history of independence, fighting, drinking, and "living one day at a time," states that he left the church after childhood and "didn't have much to do with it since then. I'm kinda a hell-raiser I guess." The implication: A hell-raiser who goes to church is a hypocrite.

These comments have a subtle ambiguity. On the one hand, there is a hostile disdain for church people, and, yet, on the other, one finds a powerfully exalted view about what the church is in itself or, at least, what it is supposed to be. These views suggest an ideal which church people so miserably fail to achieve that their very presence in the church is a hypocritical violation of what it truly is. Many hard living people are not willing or able to pay the price of such hypocrisy.

Something is terribly right about the church and something is terribly wrong. Why this is, I do not fully understand, but the people we talked with do give us some ideas about it. Part of that understanding begins with the issue of clothes.

CLOTHES

It would be difficult to overemphasize the intensity of the issue of clothing in relationship to comments about why the hard living do not go to church. When Jimmy was in the fifth grade, he reports that he was kicked out of a church he had been attending because he was wearing blue jeans. A Sunday school teacher said "unless I come back with slacks on and dress proper, I couldn't come back anymore . . . it bugged me. I didn't come back into that place until I was 17 or 16." When asked if he was angry at the entire church or at just that teacher, he replies, "Well, she represented the church." As he talked about how this event affects his belief in God, he comments: "I have a weird attitude on that. I believe in God. I don't believe in churches."

Later Jimmy reports that his daughter attends church, and he makes it clear that he does not discourage her from going, but neither will he encourage her, either. If she does go, he "will ensure that she is properly dressed."

This issue of clothing and the church comes up in a host of different ways and appears in answer to questions where one would hardly expect it. For example, one person asks Bob why he didn't belong to any church. "Hell," he answers, "I don't even own a suit!"

Another man, Gibson, comments that he did not belong to any church: "The church wouldn't care for me, the way I dress. I've probably only been there once or twice."

One of the women, who reports that she has nothing to wear to church, at one point described herself as "very masculine." In speaking proudly about her new job, Carol is pleased that she can wear her usual clothes. "I don't have to dress up. It's a good thing because I don't know how anyway."

Another woman named Charlotte reports the painful experience of children making fun of her and the clothes she wore to church. And Gibson just knows that no church would care for him given the way he dresses.

Burton spoke warmly of the way that a church helped his family when he was a boy. His mother was ill and could not work, but this church brought food and clothes. When asked if they later attended that church, Burton replies: "I don't know, we didn't hardly go to church. We didn't have clothes to go to church. We didn't have no church clothes. We didn't have nothing decent enough to go to no church. We was that bad off. We only made it one day at a time. It was a struggle."

At the very least, nice clothes are associated with going to church, so much so that one simply does not go if one cannot be properly dressed. Burton seems to appreciate the black church that stepped in to help him and his family at a time when they desperately needed it. Yet church attendance during or following that time was not an option as he saw it. "We didn't have nothin' decent enough to go to no church."

For some, like Jimmy, this relationship between clothes and church is learned at some cost. It is hard to listen to his story without feeling the stinging rebuke he received from the church. Even in his mid-forties that occasion burns in his very soul. He will *allow* his daughter to go without encouraging or discouraging her, but—and you can feel it—he will be damned if she will go without the proper attire. He cannot stand that church, but he will meet the challenge of the right clothes so that she will not endure the indignity that has scalded him for over thirty years. Clothes have become a challenge to Jimmy. They obscure any intrinsic value in church, rather it is the place where they test your worth—worse than that, where they question even your just being there—with these demeaning expectations about what one wears.

For others like Carol, wearing the right clothes requires know-how she does not possess and does not know how to get. Add that to her self-description of being "very masculine" and her sense that she really doesn't quite "fit" anywhere. Is there any condition under which she would go to a church except on a dare or, perhaps, in some extraordinary circumstance, if she got angry enough to go "just to show 'em?"

Maybe Charlotte has a better chance. Now in her mid-thirties she surely will understand that those were, after all, children who made fun of her, and that kids do that sort of thing. Clothes could not mean that much after one is in her thirties. Or does it depend on whether one has come to live in an ecology of ridicule? Do clothes then become the coagulative symbol of ice pick assaults and affronts that might not be so damaging were they not so deep, or so lasting were they not so pervasive?

Yet, I do not want to leave the impression that the clothes issue is one only of hurt and of people so broken by it all that they cannot answer the indignity without a protest of their own. Jimmy's response is, in part at least, a raised fist. Bob, who is a highly paid assembly line worker, certainly could buy a suit, but one gets the impression he is not about to do that or any number of other things that would make him eligible for respectable society. He can afford it, but he will not even grant enough credence to the mainstream conventions to become eligible, to his way of thinking, by buying a suit. Why does he not attend? "Hell, I don't even own a suit!" *And, by God, he's not going to.* He may be hurt and covering his pain, but he's mad about it, and he's not going to take it without a boycott, at least.

PREACHERS

The protest often takes place around the clergy. We heard already from Ralph's brother, Kerry, who "would knock that preacher's teeth out right now." Kerry has company in his disrespect for the ordained, if not in his violent readiness, at least in his abject disdain.

Talcott, about sixty, who is married to Helen, explains why he does not attend church. While his spouse is active, he "wasn't cut out for all that religious stuff." He believes in God but does not "see a need to be tied down to a church." He has a general respect for the church lay people, but he resents the pastor because "he has picks among the members." He only prays and visits so-called 'uppity members' who pay a lot of money to the church." Talcott came to this conclusion several years ago when Helen had been sick for a few days, and the pastor "failed to come and see her."

Jimmy, not surprisingly, certainly has no high view of religious professionals, but he makes a distinction between "preachers that when they meet you, they're glad that you're in their church. Then there's preachers that make you feel bad that you're in a church anyway." This latter group of clergy seems to be those "where all they want is the money." This was apparently hard for Jimmy when "I didn't have the money to give."

Another man, Mack, at fifty years of age was quite clear about what corrupts clergy. "What I see is wrong with a lot of churches is—especially the wealthy churches, your ministers on television—they are after the almighty dollar. The good Lord didn't intend it to be that way. The good Lord for me intended for the money that was tithed to him was to help pay the minister, the elders (if they was supposed to get paid). It was supposed to provide the minister a roof over his head and food. To me that is a part of the church. But these churches that go out—to me Oral Roberts is a perfect example, he has always been money hungry—that is not the church to me."

Others mention preachers "that holler at you," "that put you down," "that make you feel bad about being in church," and that "make you uncomfortable."

These patterned relationships between people are rituals of giving and getting respect. Our everyday practices are filled with these small liturgies, from purchasing an item at a store to mailing a package at the post office, from paying a gasoline bill at a service station, to answering a telephone. Even in highly routinized contemporary settings where a heavy flow of interaction prevents more personal comments and engagement, one can still find an efficient, professional quality that, while it is not focused on nonutilitarian friendly signals of warmth and so on can, nevertheless, convey respect as, for example, the brief interaction of a customer and a store clerk. Even the woman who sits behind the bullet-proof glass window at the service station takes my credit card, says "thank you," and calls me "sir." My answers of "Well, thank you, m'am" and "appreciate it" do not make my city the small town I grew up in, but the rituals do remind her and me that there is, after all, a person on each end of the exchange, no matter that our words lack the extended relationships of a communal existence.

With the hard living I am struck by how often these rituals either broke down or never occurred, at least not often, and this breakdown seems to be strongly felt in relation to the church and especially its clergy. In fact, the clergy seem to symbolize rituals of demeaning practices whether true or not, intentional or not, and whether these practices often occur or are actually sporadic.

Clergy, too, have bad days. They are as much at the behest of people with as few protective intermediaries as nearly any professional one can imagine, and, for the most part, they are "inexpensive" if not "free" in the cost of their services to people who choose to come through the door. After clergy have been in the ministry a while, they have been hustled by the hard living on more than a few occasions. As a result the ritual of giving and getting respect takes the liturgical form of not getting manipulated. The questions, the conversation, and the response of the pastor are more designed to check out the veracity of the man or woman who has just walked into the church, related a hardship story, and asked for help. Respect is not the ultimate issue. I know thousands of clergy, and few of them, if any, would refuse to help someone if they could be reasonably clear that they were not just being hustled.

Remember here, too, the importance of hustling to the hard living, not only as a means to cope and survive but also as a protest, as an assertion of power, as a means of "sticking it up the ass" of respectable society. With such a context these rituals of giving and getting respect do not have much chance to start with. So in a context like this, it is not surprising that "preachers" can be lightning rods. Let us then examine the critique of the clergy in this light.

In comments reported above a basic issue seems to be at

stake , although this is not exhaustive, I am sure. It is clearly an issue of class. The charge against the pastor to Talcott's spouse was that he had "picks among the members." Worse than that, really, the "picks" are the "uppity members" who give a lot of money to the church. These are the people who get the pastor's attention. This claim by Talcott takes on very pointed meaning because the preacher did not come to see his wife when she was ill. This doubtlessly was the occasion for coming to his conclusion about this particular pastor, but one misses the important place accorded *"money"* in his assertion if one hears only this one experience. We tend toward psychological interpretations in this culture, and we often obscure relations of class.

As Talcott reports his resentment, it is money, pure and simple, that makes the pastor so responsive to "uppity members." It must not be missed here that Talcott is not speaking in the aftermath of this one event only. His experiences in the highly ritualized practices of class in this society persistently take form around "money." These rituals of inequality, of giving but not getting respect, and of being demeaned, populate his life, his memory, his anger, and his resentment. For his wife, whose response he does not report and who is a good member of the church, to experience a sleight at a time of illness and need is more than enough evidence to conclude that the preacher, too, is a servant of money, his Christian preachments and his pastoral role not-withstanding. If anything, the very contradiction of the one who represents God as the one who sucks up to money does not merely cap off his experience, it redefines it with a character of hurt and ultimate cynicism. No wonder he does not attend and is not cut out for "all that religious stuff." Somehow he still believes in God, but sees no "need to be tied down to a church."

While Jimmy makes a distinction between preachers that are "glad to see you" and those "that make you feel bad," he reiterates Talcott's point about this latter group of clergy as the ones "where all they want is the money." That he "didn't have the money to give" bespeaks the living of an entire life, not a temporary shortage of funds.

Meanwhile Mack has a far better relationship to the church, as we shall see later, than either Talcott or Jimmy. It is clear to him that "the good Lord" intends that his tithe should "help pay the minister," to put "a roof over his head and food." Still, the money issue is clearly there for him. What is "wrong with a lot of churches is—especially the wealthy churches, your ministers on television—they are after the almighty dollar. The good Lord didn't intend it to be that way."

UNWANTED CHURCH

Not only the clergy but the church itself comes under serious rebuke. In some instances hard living rejection comes from the bad witness that church people make and the bad experiences they had at church, but no testimony about the church is as searing as the sheer lack of any importance whatsoever.

When Ken is asked what the church does for him, he replies, "they take my money when I send it. They keep the ole lady entertained." He is Catholic and does not "go too much," but after the comment above he retracted part of his judgment: "I shouldn't say that. The church means a lot to me. I'm not thought of too highly because I've been married twice." Yet, this last comment sounds like something he is *expected* to say. It lacks bite. One might argue that he felt excluded because of two marriages, but it seems more like relief for him in that he does not feel obligated. He said it at the beginning: "They keep the ole lady entertained."

Hardly anything gets Delton's interest, including questions about the church. He grew up in a "shack of a house." "It was never clean." In response to a question about the church, his answer is: "We couldn't go to church. Nobody liked us. To hell with that." Asked if the church could have done something had it been willing, his reply is a flat and lifeless "No." When the interviewer tries again with a question about what the church *could* do. The answer is "Nothing."

Some simply say that the church has no influence on them. Others say flatly they "have no use for the church," not in the sense that they had been hurt by it, but that it simply does not figure in their lives. One man, Donnie, says that "they never did nothing for us." There seems no edge in the comment, no hatred in the voice, simply stating the fact of the matter. George says he went to church when he was about fourteen, "but didn't like going. I didn't like sitting through sermons. Sunday school I didn't mind too much." One man, a friend of Jimmy's opines "when I became a man, I put away childish things" (then laughs).

Some have no use for the church because they had bad times there. Jerry attended a parochial school as a young child and remembers vividly a teacher who hit his left hand with a ruler every time he used it to write. He is alienated from the church now, although he maintains "a belief in a higher power."

Millie's story is quite different. "I eased out of church because there was so much common traumatic shit going on around me." While she feels some support from the church, she does not get the help she needs. She says this even as she claims that she is part of the problem. Her parents were alcoholics, and she recognizes that she closes herself off from others, associating only with those who already know about her parents' alcoholism and accepted them as such. Some of the church members themselves understand about their situation, and Millie feels that "they should have said something to my parents about what they were putting their kids through. My parents embarrassed me, and the church could have said something. They could have helped us."

Lana got involved in the church after going through some very hard times, but she had "found Christ, quit drugs, and lived on a farm." With a good job in a government service agency she had made a complete turn around in her life. Then, it happened, her next child was born with a serious birth defect, and Lana spent the next two years in and out of a hospital with her and away from the other children. Toward the end of that time her twelve year old got pregnant, and Lana did not have money for an abortion. "So I went back to illegal activities to gain the money. Yes, I went to prison. My husband wasn't there for me, and the kids thought I deserted them."

In Lana's situation it is not so much that she became disaffected with the church at that time as that life circumstances overwhelmed her, and the church was simply no longer any part of her life. Now working hard to get back on her feet after years in and out of prison she admits that she just keeps "putting it off," to go back to church. While she reports a vital faith, as we shall see later, and tries to "practice the love of the Lord" with people in the homeless shelter where she works, "I just can't see going to church. That's it. I just can't see how going to a church and sitting down makes you any more of a Christian than what you practice seven days a week."

These testimonies about the importance of the church or the lack thereof display a range of reasons for the absence of much interest at all in it. For Ken and Delton the church is virtually a nonentity. At most it is something other people do. For Donnie the church "never did nothing for us," and George did not like sitting through sermons. Jerry still resents his treatment as a left-handed student in a parochial school, and Millie believes yet that the church could have been more help than it was with her alcoholic family. Lana says she just puts off going to church, but she really sees it as extraneous to her world, even in her attempts to "practice the love of the Lord."

I am impressed here by how little the world of the church actually engages the world of these people. To be sure, one could read rationalization or bitterness or lack of discipline or something else into their comments. Perhaps they did not give the church enough credit, and perhaps some of them rejected the church so completely that even a compassionate congregation had no chance to help or support. Still, there is something more here: the church does not have practices that involve their world, that embrace and form the shape of their lives. This is where the privatization of our culture is devastating for poor and near-poor people. With privileged people who turn to the private sphere—home, church, hobbies, work—to gain energy, renewal, strength, perspective, and diversion, a congregation can program a host of opportunities to be self-selected by people in terms of preference . This may sufficiently engage such affluent people to make the church significant, at least in the private sphere, but what about people who are not privileged, who are hard living? What about people who cope to survive? Where do they find in the church the practices that are enough in touch with who they are and what they do so that the church really makes a difference, leads to some transformative action, and provides the kind of community that helps one make it through the night?

Perhaps some direction can be found here in the experience of those who have found a satisfying relation to the church, or, perhaps we can hear in the protests of hard living people something of the kind of church they would like to see. We turn first to what "the good church" or "the right church" or, as several said, what "the comfortable church" is like.

COMFORTABLE CHURCH

Ross is a biker trying to save enough money to buy another Harley. He had read a copy of *Easy Rider* when in his early teens and became increasingly interested in the biker life-style. Presently he wants to make contact with a biker minister and church in the city. While he was raised in The Covenant Church, he worshiped for a time with a Pentecostal congregation, but that didn't last long. "I liked it, but, you know, I started getting into witchcraft . . . this and that, you know, now I'm in between." He's looking for a church "in between," like the biker church. "I know the Word would be the same thing . . . you know, I've helped teach Bible studies [when he was in the Covenant Church], so I pretty well know what they're gonna have to say . . . It's just that different life-styles say it different ways. That's what I think. That's what I've been looking for. I mean, I'm not superreligious. I believe in what the Bible says, but it's hard to get into it, you know, because I go into most churches, and the first thing people see is a goatee, long hair, and tattoos . . . and I wear rings . . . plus I wear an earring at different times and I don't like [it] that . . . well, they look at me, I'm trash. I don't belong there . . . which I do. So I'm trying to find a church where I can walk into and I can feel comfortable. Once I can do that, I think life'll get a little easier. [Pause] Church ain't bad; I like it."

Ross is Charlotte's live-in. Her comments are not that different. She lists the reasons for bikers not attending church: proper attire, preachers hollering from the pulpit, preaching from the Bible in a way that cannot be understood, and lack of communication. Her ideal church would be one that "did not have a particular name." It would be "an open door church" that "didn't care how people dressed, a church that the pastor came around to visit the people."

This desire for a comfortable church is also mentioned by Mack, but he wants a church like the one his wife attends where "they treat you like family. You can go into their homes. They treat you like you was somebody. Not like you was a, shall I say, a hobo off the street."

Mack also is quite clear that church "is not necessarily in a building." It can be "in an actual church," "in a house," "in a field," "in a barn." "Church as far as I'm concerned is people getting together like at an A.A. meeting."

Again, he reiterated how much he likes his wife's church. "Although I don't drive and have any transportation, when I get a chance to go, I really enjoy the people there. They don't look down their nose at me as if to say, what the hell are you doing here?"

Of course, the issue of not being put down comes up over and over again. La Vonna is defensive, she "knew right from wrong," and she knew that while "many of the things" she did "may be wrong , it's out of necessity." Still, she wants "to find the right church," but reports that "every church I've been in so far has been full of 'perfect people' who think they are better than everybody else." More than that, the religious training for her child is important to her, but she does not want her child to feel bad about going to church without her. Apparently La Vonna will not be going with her daughter, but she fears that her child will be subjected to "put downs." Yet, she would go to a church under the right circumstances. "The church is a place where everyone should be able to find some peace of mind." La Vonna also said she "would go every Sunday if she had the proper clothing," but since she didn't, "I really should not be thought of as so bad because my heart is right."

In the hard living responses to what would be a good church, a number of other ideas received steady support. First was the idea of "a church that helps you." Jimmy wanted a church and community that would "help people with problems, where they don't lose their families. If you lose your family, you're gonna end up with someone who's a worse alcoholic than I ever thought about being." An Assembly of God church had been very helpful in Margaret's life and had become her image of what a church should be: "They were very caring people. They came around and offered help and guidance of whatever kind they could give and share. They really helped."

A second theme is the desire for an expressive church. Tony likes the black Church of God in Christ (a Pentecostal group) "because they didn't hold back. White churches are so 'practiced,' but down there they danced." An evangelical church where there is singing and clapping appeals to Gloria. "It's a lot of fun, you know." But there is also some skepticism about such expressive forms of worship. Hank observed: "You can remember when we used to go down to the Holiness Church and watch them roll around, and nine months later all the women had babies." To be fair, however, Hank's report is skewed by most accounts. One woman, who had left a mainline church went to a Pentecostal church that she enjoyed. She says: "It was never hum-drum."

The idea of sitting through a long service, especially a long sermon, one that did not get down "on my level" is a complaint that points toward a third theme. Hard living people prefer brief services that speak directly and concretely to people. Marty, for example, goes to church occasionally and especially likes the Fisherman's Mass "which only lasts twenty minutes."

Finally, a number of people mention prayer. Margaret, for instance, is quite clear about how the church might help people. She was quite clear: "People need to want to be helped first, um . . . you can go and you can knock on doors, you can call all you want, but if those people aren't ready to be reached, they won't let you. They'll shut the door in your face, hang up on you. And until they're ready . . . I don't know, just maybe a lot of prayer." She did add later in the conversation that it was important "to care about them as a person."

The needs of the hard living are confined to a short list. After the hard living indicate their expectations for churches—that are comfortable, not uppity, that fit who they are, that help you, that are open and caring, that you do not have to dress up for, that are expressive and not long and dull, and that offer prayer when nothing else works—they do not have much else to offer. When one is looking for direction from them, it becomes clear that beyond these few things, they really do not know.

One could say that they do not care, and there's some truth to this, but it is more complicated than that. The church is desperately important for those who have either been helped by it or hurt by it. One can understand why a helping and caring church would be important, but the church that is most important to the hard living is apparently the church that hurts them. It gets far more attention in their conversations, draws far more fire, and seems much more determinative in its negative impact.

Why does a hurtful church seem so visibly annoying? I think it comes from the very center of traditional approaches to providing order. Most churches who work with the poor provide traditionalist means for moving people out of disaster or chaos into some kind of disciplined ordering of their lives. There is no question that this works for some hard living people. It does not work for most, as is evident from their church participation rates. When one looks back at the issues of clothes, preachers, unwanted churches, and even the notions about what a good church is, it is clear that most hard living people "ain't buying in."

Most hard living people do not accept traditionalist approaches, and most churches that *do* work with the poor operate from this stance. The church needs yet another way. But let me be clear that I am not suggesting business-as-usual for mainstream, middle-class congregations. They are not even in the contest for reaching these people. They are virtually irrelevant to this entire question.

This issue will engage us throughout the remainder of this book. Yet, before we can approach this matter directly we must first see how the hard living understand God and the importance that this has for the central question of a hard living alternative to traditional church ministry.

4

HARD LIVING SPIRITUALITY

These people are not going to make me what they want me to be. It's not going to happen, and the things they do is null and void because He [God] has intervened in my mind." Frank is on a roll, excited, a bit angry, dead certain. He is explaining a conversation he had with God. "We talked about it. I know it sounds corny."

Yet Frank is clear that his life-style has changed "drastically" in the last five years or less. "I love the way people notice. I don't have a heathen reputation in this town. People even speak to me who used not to." Frank clarifies: "But I don't go around preaching the gospel to nobody because what I know about the Bible you could write on a notepad, a short one. But that don't mean nothing because I believe, and I believe in the power of God. And He will get me through this deal, no matter how bad I am. Because He will forgive me. He will forgive me a whole lot quicker than man. Mankind is cruel. You are branded this or branded that, and no one can erase it. So why worry about what they think. It's not what they think, it's what *He* thinks. It's what you feel and the way you present yourself.

"Me and Him [God] cut a deal. People say, 'no, no, you cut deals with the Devil.' I had a preacher say God don't make deals. I asked him when was the last time he actually sat down and had a conversation with Him, 'Did He tell you this Himself or what?' *He* [God] *told me*. I sat there and talked to Him just like I'm talking to you. If someone was here and heard this, they would lock me up or something. But it's as real as this is.

"I could be classified as one of the most nondenomic or nonreligious there is, and if you talk religion to me I get mad, real mad."

Frank had gone through a lot of hard living by his own report and the report of friends present during this conversation. His statement is rich in its display of hard living spirituality. First, he believes in the immediate and personal involvement of God in his life, an involvement that results from his having "cut a deal" with the deity. This conviction about God's providence, for those who believe, is perhaps the single most persistent theme in hard living spirituality.

Second, as was indicated in the last chapter, the separation of one's spiritual life, one's belief in God from participation in the church, is sharply underscored in Frank's remarks. He is one of the most "nondenomic [meaning nondenominational], nonreligious" persons there is. Talk of religion—read this as institutional, traditional church religion—makes him "mad, real mad." To be sure, this separation between belief and church participation has been prominent in the life-styles of post-World War II baby boomers, and Frank, in his thirties, is one, but hard living beliefs antedate this more recent trend. While people such as Frank may be influenced by his generation's views, this separation among the hard living has its more profound sources in the chaotic relations of their lives rather than in the institutional disillusionment of the more recent trend among affluent, estranged baby boomers whose counter-cultural propensities most exemplified it.

Actually, hard living views of the church and spirituality are of two broad kinds, one that does, indeed, find expression in the church and the other, like Frank's view, that wants to remain distant from *any* such traditional, institutional practice.

Finally, for now, Frank has an embattled sense of his own

independence and freedom. "These people are not going to make me what they want me to be." At one point in the conversation a friend reminds Frank that other people regard him as "just an outlaw trucker." It was this comment that "set him off" and brought out his angry refutations of their opinions, that "it's not what *they* think, but what *He* [God] thinks." Then he follows immediately with the comment that "it's what *you* feel and how you present yourself."

These three characterizations I have made about Frank's comments are not meant to encapsulate hard living spirituality, because their views about God and their relationships to God are enormously complex. As I worked with the stories the hard living told us, however, these three characteristics seemed to be a part of almost every conversation we had with the few exceptions noted. The best place to begin is with a virtually pervasive sense of the providence of God among the hard living.

GOD'S PROVIDENCE

Agnes grew up in a middle-class family and attended a suburban church. Her parents divorced, and she spent most of her time in day care. Sometime during these years she rebelled and started doing drugs, a practice that soon landed her in juvenile detention and significant trouble. As she moved into her late teens, what began as rebellious experimentation with drugs became serious addiction to alcohol, cocaine, and whatever else was available when these were not. She reports blackouts that lasted for days, even weeks. She remembers wanting "to make the world as bad as I felt." In those years she remembers believing there was "a God, but not one for me."

One day Agnes had been blacked out for days and had seriously overdosed. Her live-in, whom she says she genuinely loved and who was at least her equal as a drug abuser, was standing over her yelling, telling her that she "was in deep shit" and had to get help. Somehow they managed to get her help, and soon thereafter she entered a detox center, got sober, and has been so ever since. Her live-in followed her later into the same center, joined A.A., and never used drugs again. He was, however, killed in an industrial accident after about a year of sobriety.

Agnes was completely stunned, of course, by his death. "This wasn't supposed to happen. This was not in the program for recovery. How could this be?" Somehow she managed to remain drug-free even through this time by attending A.A. meetings once and twice a day and by working hard in the detox center. Three years later she says: "I don't believe anything happened that wasn't in God's plan."

This understanding that even the worst things that happen are God's will and within divine providence is something one hears repeatedly among the hard living. The temptation for someone like me is to dismiss such views as narcotic, that this is not "truly healthy" or "authentic" faith but rather a belief that anesthetizes those in great pain so that they can continue to live, albeit numbed. My typical suspicion is that such views tend, also, to insulate people from life, assuaging them with some "supernatural economy" that makes everything okay, though the perspective does not actually enable one to affirm life and face it with a courage that does not need such fictions. I usually want people to have something like what Tillich called "the courage to be," the capacity to take on these fundamental threats in human affairs and not be overcome by them.

Yet, quite frankly, I am suspicious of my suspicions. I know that religion can be an opiate, and that some damaged souls do escape into a "religious bubble" to thwart the pain of the world, but I am convinced that one cannot determine this alone by what people *say*. One must also ask about the *practices* of people who hold such view. How does that language come into play in daily life? How is the language *used*? Indeed, what happens in the relationship between their *talk* and their *walk*? Before we decide, for example, that Agnes' faith in God's providence is narcotic, let us take note of what she has *done* these past few years. She went back to school, to college, to pursue a degree in counseling while she continued to work with alcoholics and other drug abusers on a day-to-day basis. Along with all these responsibilities she continues her A.A. meetings, working diligently to stay sober one day at a time. Is this narcotic? Hardly.

But perhaps we need to see someone who is not so successful. We met Lana before in the last chapter, where she had responded to a newly-born daughter's birth defect at the hospital only to come up against the fact of her twelve-year old's pregnancy. Her move into illegal activities to get money for an abortion landed her in jail. Two things, however, seem quite important in this context. She responded in anger to the child with the birth defect. Lana reports that at first she "Cussed 'Him up there' [God] a lot. I couldn't understand why He would give me this child. I did drugs through my other children. My last child I didn't. I was going to church faithfully and became pregnant and carried her. Did nothing wrong, and He gives me a child that is not normal . . . She [her daughter] had a lot of problems and I couldn't understand what I had done to deserve this. And, yeah, I cursed Him a lot."

"The preacher," from the church she attended began to call her at the hospital long distance, especially when her daughter was in surgery. "And he kept saying that 'this is not your child. Why are you cursing over something that is not yours?' I said, 'It is mine.' He said, 'no, it is not. It is God's child. No matter whether He takes her now or when she gets eighty, no matter, she is God's child. He is loaning it to you to love, to nurture, to teach, but it is not yours.' Oh, he preached this to me for about six months. Once I realized this, if she died, so what. I mean it's not 'so what,' but it was given to me. Then I eased a lot in my mind. I handled death real well. Death is nothing."

Interviewer: "Did this child die?"

"No, it seems like when I accepted this, He [God] made her well. The preacher kept saying: 'The Lord gives you no more than you can bear.' Sometimes you wonder, but He will not give you any more than He thinks you can bear. I used to always say that I could never handle a child that was deformed or wasn't normal. I would see a child that wasn't normal, and I would say 'Oh, God, I would have to put it in a home.' You know I couldn't deal with it. That was my big hang up that my kids was all beautiful and healthy and smart. I said I couldn't deal with it. Well, I did deal with it. He made me."

It is true that she turned to criminal activity toward the end of this time to get enough money for her daughter's abortion. Given the constraints under which Lana lived, however, this does not dent finally her testimony about her own faith in God's providence. In fact, having completed her time in prison, she now works in a homeless center where, as she says, she tries "to practice the love of the Lord."

My point here is that in each of these cases the conviction about God's providence did not anesthetize these women from life but, in fact, helped them face it. They did not use such belief to hide from challenges before them but, indeed, as a reason to take them on and assume responsibility for them. The fact is that whether a religious view is narcotic or not cannot be determined only by what is said but by how it is used and the meanings and practices that relate to it which may or may not be explicitly contained in the statement itself. More than this, such statements of religious faith must be seen in their contexts and how these meanings and practices function in the midst of chaos.

LIFE OUT OF CONTROL

Rexine Bryant is a pastor who serves in a hard living community in Wichita, Kansas. At the time of our conversation I was having difficulty trying to understand what was going on with the people who believed God willed even the day-to-day events of their lives. Rexine spoke directly to the matter. "Tex, these people see their lives as out of their control. They see their lives as effects, not causes. For them to understand that everything is God's will is the only hope of some kind of stability they have in their entire lives." She also raised a second matter. "You see, Tex, if God is in control, then they have someone who can really change things. God can be approached through prayer or some other way. In fact, God can then be bargained with and won over, as they see it."

It is easy to forget what it means to live with life out of control. Obviously, life is not finally in control for any of us. A lump on the rib cage, a strange discharge of blood, a sudden excruciating chest pain, a fatal stroke, a hurricane, an accident; any of these and more, can bring all of us quite suddenly up against the radical fragility of life. So in this sense, no one has life under control.

Take my own situation. I am a tenured, full professor in a theological school. Unless I am found guilty of moral turpitude, refuse to do my duties, become incompetent, or am otherwise incapacitated, my job is unusually secure. Even if my school should collapse financially, I am apparently guaranteed a clergy appointment in a parish or other setting within The United Methodist Church. Beyond these even, I have Social Security and a pension that I *could* live on if worse came to worse. My intention here is not boastful. It is rather to point out the difference between my situation and that of the person who virtually has nothing and is an illness or a paycheck away from financial disaster. Or, what about a woman who makes $7,000 a year and is married to a man who makes $15,000? What happens to her if he dies or takes a walk? She is immediately poor and confronted with a new range of issues for which she is completely unready in material terms.

When life is out of control, the assertion that everything is designed according to a divine plan can lead one to a strange, powerful, and ultimate sense of security and safety. Out of this one discovers a heavy duty to perform, the need for a compassionate response to the world as a more faithful expression of one's life, having now gone through a foreordained prodigality and wild wandering that led one to this time and place in the economy of God. This happens with

hard living people. Even for those caught in the miasmic swirl
of drug abuse, it may be the last vestige of hope.

CODE LANGUAGE

Hard living assertions about faith in God's providence will
be best understood if they are seen as code language. By this I
do not mean secretive phrases and statements which they
communicate with each other and vouchsafe only to themselves. I mean simply that such language should not be read
literally and certainly not in a systematic way, because the
words carry far richer and much more complicated meaning
than what they signify on the surface.

People who use these providential claims have many ways
to make exceptions to otherwise flat assertions, so that they
can nuance their own understanding. For example, Tony, who
believes firmly in God's immediate providential care had a far
more complex understanding of God's work than may appear
on the surface. He reports that his mother told him, "God
didn't mean the easy way out for you" after Tony had done a
robbery. She said: "God didn't let you get away with robbery."
And Tony agrees: "That first robbery messed me up bad. I will
never do it again. I was wired up in jail without the comforts of
home . . . had to have food shot in between my teeth into my
mouth."

Now, if you said to Tony, Why would God will that you not
get "the easy way out" after God, on your view, had willed
that you actually do the robbery? Tony's response to this
contradiction would be simple, "That's not what I was
saying."

Such code language is not meant to be taken in a literal way.
It is not an attempt to make a theological statement in a critical,
systematic, discursive sense; rather it is a religious affirmation
that has a host of meanings, many of which have no necessary
analytical implication in the assertion. Such affirmations relate
to a wide variety of settings and encode instruction, guidance,

support, and affirmation which are tacitly understood but never articulated in any full-blown systematic point of view.

Yet, the language is more than that too. Talk of miracles, reports of God's active intervention in day-to-day life, testimonies of sudden cures, changes of fortune, release from a certain fate: While these may be intensely believed, they are also ways to claim transcendence. Their purpose is not to lay out a rationally defensible set of propositions but a way of accounting for the concrete lived events in their lives as visited by One who will finally set all things straight. One man said: "God bats last."

This belief in immediate providence is not distanced from "what's happening," but rather understands God to be concretely involved in life. If someone dies or does not die, if someone recovers from illness or does not, if something good happens or something evil, those who believe in this Providential Presence have more than enough encoded complexity in their understanding, tacit though it may be, to account for the unpredictability of their lives. In fact, some, as we have seen, draw from it a durable courage and staying power that will test the mettle of anyone whose theology is more discursively defensible.

PROVIDENCE AS PROTEST

The tradition in thought that sees religion as an opiate had perhaps its most powerful exponents in the early Feuerbach and the young Marx. One problem with both these thinkers was their lack of appreciation and interest in popular culture. Marx, for example, would place most hard living people in the *lumpenproletariat*. They were extraneous to the tides of history moving toward freedom and a communist society. To the early Feuerbach and the young Marx there was no genuine mystery in such people, hence neither of them could "hear the music." Such views do not look closely enough, and hence are unreliable as a means of clarifying the religious lives of the poor and the near poor.

Michel de Certeau reports studies of peasants and the role of religious hope in the powerlessness of their lives. In the "immemorial struggle" between "the powerful" and "the poor" these studies found that the poor parted space into two spheres. One space was the socioeconomic, where the rich and the police always won, and where mendacity reigned. In this space, the strong always triumph, and words always deceive. At a Renault automobile factory in Billancourt, near Paris, where many North African immigrants work, a Maghrebian syndicalist said it pointedly: "They always fuck us over."

Yet, there was always another sphere, a utopian space, "in which a possibility, by definition miraculous in nature, was affirmed by religious stories. While peasants faced a pervasive injustice not only from the powers that be but from history itself, they accepted this as *fact* but *not as the way things were supposed to be*. This disjointing of fact and meaning found expression in religious worldviews where the supernatural "by means of celestial landmarks, creates a place for this protest," an *ethical* declaration (p. 16). The unacceptable presence of the established powers was attested through the vision of miraculous intervention. In this sphere hope could be maintained, because "life cannot be reduced to what one sees of it." This miraculous truth telling is more, much more, than the specific religious beliefs that are its metaphoric and symbolic expression. Here miracles create another space, which coexists with that of an experience deprived of illusions.

It is my conviction that far too much of the study of the poor has interpreted falsely their religion and spirituality as an opiate, as a narcotic escape from the world. While this is not absent in the people we talked with, a far more adequate interpretation is one that sees their views of God and their spirituality as protest. The spirituality of the hard living does create "another sphere," "a utopian space," really an entire economy of God where things will finally be what they are supposed to be. Life *is* more than what one sees. God's will *is* being done. Most hard living people do not have illusions about the ragged, gashing edges of life; in fact, they know what it is to be "up against the wall."

I am not suggesting that those with chemical addictions do not use these as opiates, although even here I sense in drug use a protest that cannot be reduced to narcotic purposes alone. Yet, their religious claims, even in the depths of drug abuse, open a place for hope, a protest of their condition, and yes, an objection to a conventional order that wants to make them something they are not. To reduce such people to sniveling refugees from the world in some anesthetized spirituality is to engage in an abstraction divorced from the thick description of the lives of people who, if they do not know how to do anything else, know how, by God, to fight.

When God Fails

It would be a falsification of the testimonies of the hard living to suggest that all of them believe in the providence of God. Some clearly do not. Their alienation from God (or their outright disbelief in a Deity) is usually proportionate to their rejection of the larger society. Those who did not hold to God's providence were of four kinds.

The first group at one time believed in God's providential care, but this fell into serious question by the turn of events in their lives. Cheryl divorced a violently abusive husband after a dozen years of marriage and lost custody of their son and daughter. She reports that even if it did cost her the children, she had to leave. Her husband had a drinking problem and, when intoxicated, beat her. She suffered cuts, bruises, and, sometimes, broken bones. Too embarrassed to go to work, she would be fired for missing.

Cheryl says that "everybody calls me a survivor. Well, I'm sick of surviving. Why does God do this to me? Why does He let this happen? Why doesn't He stop this." Obviously, Cheryl's complaint assumes that the events of her life are God's will. This, of course, is the problem for some who believe in such a direct providence. When things go bad, God takes the blame, and a serious crisis of belief occurs.

Anna's problems with God grew from the deaths of three family members within the space of a single year. "All this together destroyed my world." She describes herself as "lost," and as "extremely angry with God. He took away everything, and I hate him for it." When all this happened, she began running the streets and became "a bad girl."

A second type of response, which is not necessarily exclusive of the others, is one which sees life as a battleground between God and Satan. Matt, for example, believes in God, but he also listens "to other voices," which come from Satan. "If I were a better person, I wouldn't hear the voices, or at least I wouldn't be controlled by them." These voices tell him that he's going to die of his liver disorder, and this scares him.

In listening to Matt, one gets the impression that Satan is more powerful than God, or, at least, that God is so much more distant than the immediacy of Satan's threats and temptations. Someone explains to Matt that God understands how hard it is to believe and that it is okay to doubt. It is because of Jesus' coming to earth that God knows what it's like to live in the world, to be tormented by things you cannot control, and to hear voices. With this comment Matt leaned forward, suddenly quite alert and says: "Do you really believe that? Nobody ever told me that before. I thought God must think I'm really bad. Does God really know how bad it is?"

A third group of people are quite ambivalent about God. Carol tried membership with the Jehovah's Witnesses and then with the Baptists, where she "had the Bible literally beaten over my head," but life has taken her in a different direction. "If I wrote a book," she claims, "nobody would believe it because it's too real. That's the problem." Her unusual experiences take her to strange places in her thoughts as well, including her religious beliefs. "I dabbled in black magic and scared myself. I think right now I basically believe on the lines, border lines of voodoo. I believe in nature and the old saying, 'Shit happens.' You just got to keep on trucking. I will survive."

Todd also is quite mixed in his understanding about God and his beliefs. He is clear that he does not want any relationship with the church although he admits that it "has a magic that works, I just don't want it." He reports: "I found God by accident trying to stay out of prison," where he had spent ten years before he was thirty-two years old. His discovery of God came not through his experience of having been raised in the church, but rather through Alcoholics Anonymous. Todd has found God through the twelve-step program. There he met "a personal, private God, and I fight with Him. I'm pissed off because I wasted ten years in prison and in drug abuse." He wonders why life threw him such a curve and why his church experience was so bad where he heard so much about a judgmental, vengeful God.

Even while A.A. has been crucial in his struggle for sobriety and in finding God, Todd confesses that he really doesn't "want to know God's will very much." "The most trouble I have in A.A. is surrender. I'm afraid God is fucking around in Brazil somewhere and not here."

A final group, and this list is suggestive not exhaustive, are those for whom God simply is not a reality at all. It is a small number of people, but their views are decidedly clear and forthright. Some were raised in the church, and even report they "didn't mind it," but George captures the essence of their views in one line. "I don't really believe in God or anything." One can conjecture why these few have no such belief in the face of such pervasive testimony by so many to the contrary. In George's case he has a long history of violence. He shot, but did not kill, three men. He has a prison record, a serious drinking problem that goes back to high school days, and a violent temper, but he is not unique in these. He is now working hard to control his drinking and experiences "some success" this past year. Moreover, he is not poor, but, in fact, he owned a bar where much of his "trouble" occurred. He "just doesn't believe in God or anything."

Yet, the overwhelming majority of the hard living profess belief in God, especially for a providential God in charge of the ebb and flow of their lives. As stated above, however, most do not go to church, although a few do. This relationship, or lack of it, to the church takes several quite distinct expressions. A closer look at these will extend our understanding of hard living spirituality. I specifically want to examine these in relation to two different "worlds."

5

A HALF STEP FROM HELL

Look, there ain't but two places for us: You either live in hell or you live a half step away," Rob exclaimed after I described the hard living. Yet, the more I reflected on his simple and graphic comment, the more it characterized what so many hard living people represent. Furthermore, hard living relationships to the church are profoundly shaped by these two different, but ever so close, worlds!

The "in hell" group typically is caught in the throes of drug/alcohol abuse, and all of life for the abuser is oriented toward getting a "fix." Even if one has a job, one's salary or wages "evaporate" in alcoholic binges or the exorbitant costs of illegal drugs. The family of the drug/alcohol abuser is held hostage by the scandal, the unpredictability, the marginality, the powerlessness, the poverty of their lives before the certainties of his or her compulsiveness and the chaos wrought by it. In the case of the abuser, life is lived between the poles of being high and the unmanageable ache of jangled nerves and the mounting urgency for the relief that means everything. The desperation of the family of the abuser and his or her seismic weariness of the addiction—becoming sick and tired of being sick and tired, which may be the only hope—constitute a hell that is worse than hot and a disaster deeper than the devastation of untimely death.

The plight of those "a half step away" has its own tedious

and unending exaction in the day-to-day coping with a life where the money is always tight, and the demands of work and family and just living are incessant. If the abuser is now recovering, every morning becomes that uncertain quest to meet a continual challenge to stay sober today. For the family, theirs is the bittersweet of his or her sobriety, on the one hand, and the muffled wondering, on the other, about what might have been had the family not suffered from all the years of lost income, squandered opportunities, and the wounds that even yet have the inelastic scars of injuries too deep to heal right.

But not all people, not even most who live "a half step away," are families with drug abusers. Far more numerous are those who struggle to make ends meet and to find religious strength and a stalwart morality that can stem the eroding ties of families where there is never quite enough, where the work is monotonous and deadening; where one feels the necessity day by day to tell the children "no," they cannot have this or that, and besides they don't need it, when, in fact, the family cannot afford it. Their conventional moralities are the hard-pressed wisdom of a world where the sustenance of some semblance of order against the chaos comes from staying on the straight and narrow because life, even now, is too expensive for the money and too demanding for the energy.

THE RESPECTABLE CHURCH

As we talked to the hard living these two worlds emerged over and over again, and with them three quite distinct responses to the church. The first response is the one less likely to occur, but it clearly does happen. This pattern is the one most likely to be found in mainline churches. It is more typical of women than men, as is all church attendance among the hard living and other classes for that matter, and involves almost always the family member who is not drug dependent or at least is now recovering. They often are active in respectable neighborhood churches that support conventional moralities and family values. These churches play an important stabilizing role in helping people keep things together through the community life and activities they provide. These are a people who live "a half step from hell," knowing that it would not take much to disrupt the meager hold they have on life. These people are without exception, courageous people who meet the unrelieved stresses and the everyday difficulties of their lives with strength and hope. They tell you that they "could not do it without the Lord."

Beatrice has been a member of the church all her life, moving from an Assembly of God to a Baptist and then to a United Methodist church. She has been a Sunday school teacher, a member of the women's group, and the chair of the education program in the last congregation where she has belonged for more than a quarter of a century. Her husband who had severe drinking problems early on in the marriage cannot now work due to crippling arthritis in his knees. Together they have four children, and they have struggled throughout their entire lives. The children are grown, and Beatrice and her husband managed to buy a small $25,000 house in an old residential working-class neighborhood. Making the payments, caring for the children, holding the family together during his drinking years, and even now being the major source of the household income, Beatrice describes herself as "in control," one who "rarely comes unglued." Her husband says "she has ice water in her veins."

Their fourth child was mentally handicapped. To Beatrice her son's problems "were a special task from God." She had major illnesses as a child but believed she "had been spared for a reason." Her special son was that reason, and caring for him "gives meaning to my life." Beatrice believes that God chooses a person for a "special burden," and she is living out God's will and calling for her. She sees her life as valuable and contributing to God's plan. "The Lord helps me a lot," she added. "He gives me lots of strength to get through each day."

A faithful, steady church member all her life, her husband seldom attends. His recent health problems "have scared him," however, and "he is asking questions about faith. I wish he would go to church with me so we could participate in activities together."

THE SECT-LIKE CHURCH

A second group of hard living find their way into traditional sect-like churches with clear, fixed, unambiguous certainties about what is right and wrong and about what must be believed in order to be saved. These are people under economic threat and cultural dismissal. They seek an island of certainty in a sea of unpredictability. Such people are often ridiculed and categorized by reduction as judgmental, hardheaded, insensitive, simpleminded authoritarians who have no understanding of the complexities of moral life. Such views fail to see that these are embattled, often forgotten people, who turn to faith and morality to build fortresses against marauding economic and social disasters that split marriages, get children into trouble, place families at risk before the exorbitant costs of the legal system, forfeit a mortgage—if they are fortunate enough to have one—and shut down the gaunt opportunities for their progeny who are the bearers of their hopes. Their children represent the survivors of parental dreams, dreams long since crashed on the realities of structured social inequality and socialized failure.

Judy heard about this book from her pastor. She asked if she could write me and share her views. Her letter so represents the sect-like view that it appears below in its unedited entirety:

MY HISTORY

After having lived for forty-three years and traveled over most of the U.S.A. I feel I have a basic understanding of hard living and the people that make up this segment of society. I have sinned against God in every area of his commandments.

From murder (called abortion by liberals) to drug and alcohol addiction (called fun by the ignorant). I can and will go into details if anyone wants to know. My attitude about sin and punishment were formed in early childhood. Framed by sexual and physical abuse from my Dad and mental and emotional abuse from my Mother, my sense of self esteem was so badly damaged it took me twenty-three years to overcome it. I still have my moments but God has restored my inborn sense of right and wrong and now I know I can turn to Him in his word for guidance.

THE CHURCH

So many times since I was saved I tried to turn to the church for help and guidance and was disappointed at every turn by the attitudes of Pastors and teachers. Christian people seemed to be judgmental of my lifestyle, uncaring of my needs, and totally oblivious of their failure to carry out the great commission. The lukewarm church of Laodicea was and is a reality to me. I have made a vow to not be lukewarm in my dealing with people. God has not allowed me to forget Matthew 25: 31-46. I perceive that ignoring this teaching is the worst failure of any Christian congregation. With as many businessmen and apparently wealthy people as we have in the churches, there is no excuse for unemployment in a congregation of Gods people. There is no excuse for people in our churches to be without basic needs. Yet we have people in our midst who don't come to church because they don't have the right clothes, because they don't have soap to wash, because they feel uncomfortable with people who don't have sin in their lives. Matthew 23:27. If any Christian thinks they are fooling the unbelievers they better think again. Street people and children see through any form of hypocrisy almost immediately. Without any bible teaching they judge us better by Gods standards than we judge ourselves. Our members seem to have the ability to put on blinders when we see things we don't want to deal with.

We have a decided tendency to be to busy, to rich, to poor, to ignorant, to of anything to get involved in really helping fulfill needs in our churched and unchurched brethren.

To do Gods will should be the first priority of any proclaiming Christian. If we are willing God will make us able. If we live by faith it becomes very apparent to people in our area of influence.

Hard living people are always looking for a way out of their circumstances. If the church is content to let them think that money is the answer then the church is not of God but of man. Money is only part of the answer. Paul teaches in Ephesians 4:11- 13 what we need to know. We can't teach this principle without living it. We lose the hard living people because we don't practice what we preach. Lately we don't even preach. We go through the motions and wonder why we don't get anything out of our Christian life except busyness. Now that I have gotten under Gods authority (at least some of the time) I see rewards for being there. In living by the faith I so loudly proclaim I have a real life for the first time. In studying Gods word with a grateful spirit I am continually learning more of Gods will and of his blessings for obedience. He is making me into a hard living, joy filled, thankful, contented Christian. In my perception, this is what he wants for all of us. I'm still not rich in worldly things. I still sin against God. I still have lapses in my faith. But God is providing for my needs. In sharing with others what God has given me I learn more about Gods Salvation, Grace, and Glory. I guess I'll make a list of stuff we need to do as professing Christians to bring in hard living people and teach them to be hard living Christians.

BE ATTITUDES

1. Be honest
2. Be caring
3. Be willing
4. Be careful
5. Be understanding
6. Be gentle
7. Be honest
8. Be faithful
9. Be considerate
10. Be honest
11. Be hospitable
12. Be ready
13. Be responsible
14. Be unselfish
15. Be honest
16. Be forgiving

When we give someone a coat it should be one of our best coats, not our throw-a-ways. God gives us His best. Should we do less? Don't look for material rewards for doing Gods will. Our rewards are stored in heaven. God is no respecter of persons, neither should we be.

And in all of this I'm always open to discussion and issue an open invitation to my home which God provides.

The third response of the hard living is decidedly against involvement in the church. If women tend to be more involved in respectable and sect-like churches than the men, then the opposite is the case here, although women can be found in this third alternative. This pattern seems to be a complex of factors, some of which seem highly charged and others seem more matter of fact or obvious. Consider these four factors.

The first characteristic of this pattern is an insurrectionary disdain for anything the church does that smacks of demeaning treatment of the hard living. Jo Ann, who earlier told us that she simply did not believe in God, also said that if she could "get a job and some of the right clothes" she might "give the church a try" to see if she could discover "what all the fuss about God was all about." She is, however, very proud and made it abundantly clear that she would "not allow anybody to put me down" for anything she had said or done. If she went into church and ran into that she would say, " 'the fuck with it' and leave."

A second characteristic is the conviction that the church is trying to do something to them and therefore has to be carefully watched and resisted. For some this suspicion is raised by preachers and money. In talking about the church Pit Bull indicated that he had "nothing against the church, it's just not for me." Sometimes, though, the church is "just a scam to make some preacher rich." He figured he was "too smart to be taken in by the bullshit that's fed to people in the churches."

We easily forget that the hard living frequently experience institutions doing something *to* them. Whether it be in uneven employment, welfare organizations, homeless shelters, detox centers, stores, cafes, and so forth, the church is one place they "do not have to put up with it" and they don't.

A third factor seems to be related to the help some of the hard living receive from the church and their perception that an expectation of indebtedness comes with the assistance. Jimmy is especially sensitive to this issue. A friend of his named Ron has "a mental problem" and got into trouble. Jimmy bailed him out and gave him a place to stay in Jimmy's house. "He'll never be able to pay it back . . . because he can't hold a job. It's stress . . . and it bothers him. But like I told him I'd rather him owe me than somebody that's gonna force him into paying it back right away." Someone asked if Jimmy is talking about "giving without any strings." "Right," he says, "you can help people and not make them feel like they owe you one." Jimmy knows that a gift that incurs debt is a clear message to the receiver: "I'm better than you; you're below me." He notes why "a lot of churches are like that," and he says that "if you go to church [for help], they think you owe them." Jimmy cannot fathom why the church could not give as freely as he had to Ron.

In this same vein, Talcott is asked: "If you could request anything from the church where your wife attends and be assured of getting it, what would you ask for?" Talcott chuckles at the question and bargains, "Well, that would depend on what I would have to do to get it." When told that there is nothing that he has to do, he breaks up in loud and sarcastic laughter.

A fourth factor is the activities of the church and a lack of "fit" with this particular group of hard living people. Sometimes this problem is mixed up with lack of money. Mack complains about a church he once attended because "most of the functions was expensive." But Marty, a Catholic, who does attend mass regularly does not go to functions: "I'm not real big on activities at the church. I don't mix well with crowds." Many of the others, especially men say things such as: "I'm not religious," "I'm not cut out for that," "That's not my thing," "I don't need it," and so on.

Evidently the practices which make up the lives of these

hard living people are radically discontinuous with those of the church, both the mainline, conventional kinds of church and those more sect-like. I do not only mean here their practices of drug use, carousing, parties, and hell raising. It is more pervasive than these. I suggest that it encompasses the entirety of their lives for reasons that will become apparent as we move into the last section of the book.

THE CHURCH AND THE WILD SIDE

We have seen several times now the ways in which hard living people defiantly maintain their individual freedom and independence. "I ain't gonna take no shit" and "nobody better not fuck with me." Unusual is the hard living person who does *not* make such claims.

A deep contradiction permeates these declarations, especially for those in bondage to profoundly destructive drug addictions. Bravado about such personal sovereignty by someone whose major preoccupation is the next "fix" sounds hollow indeed. And yet, one looks at what they have been through: their upbringing, the endless struggle, their capacity to make it on the street, to dodge the police, in some cases to survive prison, to live under bridges and in flophouses, to move from apartment to broken down apartment, to manage a rainfall of assaults on their dignity, and all of this doubtlessly in some cases attributable, at least in part, to a genetic thirst for narcotic chemicals. Is there not here even in all their vulnerability, a durable objection of humanity against the world? I wonder what on earth they would be or could do if there were not that crude moment of protest that is captured in what is finally the last best play in a bad hand of cards: "Fuck you."

What has become so clear in these interviews and in my going over them time and again is how important a role protest and rebellion play in their lives. Their commitment to "the wild side of life" is basic to that protest. As destructive as it can be, and usually is in its violence and drug abuse, it is the one thing they have left.

It is not strange, then, that they have so much trouble with the church. I have come to realize that the church has basically three options for the hard living (and I don't include the affluent middle-class congregation). The affluent church can provide mostly charity. Virtually none of its members would tolerate their presence. The arctic reception would freeze the most dauntless hard living heart. Even the gentle middle-class souls of hospitality would be tripping on their habits of toleration, not unlike the priest struggling to play softball in his cassock.

Those conventional, respectable churches such as the one Beatrice attends may touch a few, but their practices are too ordinary, too lacking in excitement, and too absent of the practices that could manage a significant and effective ministry, at least in those terms.

In the past the most successful churches in reaching the poor have been the traditional, sect-like churches which contain people like Judy, who announce their stringent morality, sharp identity, and true believing army that is doing battle against Satan's principalities and powers. Even yet, they can reach great numbers of the poor and, today, especially in Pentecostal form, they touch more hard living lives than any other church.

But none of these will work with the hard living who are in sharpest protest against the church, and the reason is abundantly clear, but we do not see it because it is too close. The institutional frameworks and practices of both the respectable and the sect-like churches are organized to deal with the chaos and disorder of lives. This is key to their ministry and, indeed, their effectiveness. If persons will give themselves to these communal congregations built to withstand the ominous threats of a world out of control, one can usually make it, even with struggles such as Beatrice had. However, a key factor in both the respectable church and the sect-like one is the element of control. These churches are designed to curb passions and to bring people into line with a socially and morally conservative approach to family, work, school, children, neighborhood, and country.

Basic to the approaches of both these types of churches is the attempt to bring the wayward, those who live on the wild side of life, into line. The wild side of life is the greatest threat for a family living close to economic and interpersonal bankruptcy: The money for the booze and the drugs, the carousing and its continual threat to the marriage, the inattention to the children or outright meanness toward them, the bonding and partying with friends outside and beyond family relationships—friends who themselves are in trouble with *their* spouses, their children, their jobs, the courts, with somebody or something, somehow, somewhere.

The stock in trade of these churches is to deal especially with male social behavior and its ever present threat to traditional life and its tenuous grip on stability. Country music, for example, is full of descriptions of such men and their problems with family, love, work, children, life, and even the good Lord. Take Willie Nelson's advice: "Mamas Don't Let Your Babies Grow Up to Be Cowboys." His song about "The Good Hearted Woman in Love With a Good Timing Man." His plea: "Whiskey River Take My Mind You're All I Got to Take Care of Me." The preoccupation in country music with lost love, the battle between the sexes, the party life, the hard drinking, the fighting, job troubles, being broke, the loss of a good wife and beloved children, the regret, the unrecoverable yesterday, the tomorrow filled with pain and without hope, and the today "that ain't what it used to be." There is no question that this music is written for commercial purposes, but it is also written for those who believe that it sings their songs, and it vibrates with the episodic lived stories of no few hard living people in the United States.

Men are exceptionally prone to the disruptive practices of this life-style, but women, too, can more than live out the wild side of life, and country music has a central theme of "the good girl gone bad." The woman of Loretta Lynn's song "The Pill" is now going to get herself a miniskirt, not a maternity dress, and she's going to have some fun herself and check out all the places her husband's been while she has been home and pregnant. One is struck by the fact that in country music, women have basically two options: they can be good girls, good wives, good mothers, good daughters, or they can go bad. This may be closer to the realities of class and more significant insight than country music is usually given credit for.

Basic to the calling and the practices of the respectable and the sect-like churches is control of the hard living on the wild side of life, especially of the men. The holiness of these churches about smoking, drinking, cursing, bad habits, the partying spirit, misusing money, and so on takes direct aim at hard living. The invitation is extended to spend major amounts of time at the church in its family-oriented programs. Practices that discipline husband, wife, and children to pray together, read the Bible together, and go to church together are designed to resist the chaotic disruptions of temptation. The conviction that the ways of the world are not to be trusted but opposed outright, while moderated in the more accommodated respectable churches, declares spiritual warfare against the enemies of the family, home, and church. Often, especially in the sectarian church, one finds religious teaching where clearly the armies of God and the forces of evil are joined in mortal combat with no question about the final outcome which is usually seen as coming soon. The urgency of decision, the cosmic importance of a changed life, the clear implications and benefits for family, and its unavoidable eternal implications: All these and more call the sinner to come home "just as I am."

For many people this message has been the difference literally between life and death. Millions of families have turned from chaos to some semblance of order. It has made marriages work and kept children from the destructive practices their parents previously lived. It has balanced the home budget and provided an existence that by most counts has been simply more liveable. To be sure, one finds here hypocrisy, self-righteousness, arrogant presumption of truth, and the racism and sexism so abounding *throughout* our culture, but these are among the deepest of all our sins and can hardly be scapegoated on those who struggle most.

In fact, I doubt that the poor and near-poor contribute nearly as much to the systemic violation of white females and the ethnic men and women of our culture as do those of us who as privileged elites make decisions, formulate policy, and continue the institutional mobilization of bias that are far more pervasive in impact, even if sometimes less directly joined, to the fates of those marginal to established power. And can one really say that the poor and the near-poor are more arrogant, more presumptive of the truth, and more hypocritical than the elites who are "the brightest and the best" or the "supply siders" and "free-enterprisers?" Really? More so than the Johnson, Nixon, Reagan and Bush administrations and the Democratic congresses that gave us Vietnam, Watergate, a trillion and a half dollars of military debt, leveraged buy-outs, welfare to the rich, and a ravaged domestic economy—while talking about "a thousand points of light?" One of the hard living men raging about these very things simply said, "Shit."

THE CHURCH GAME AND THE COUNTER GAME

There is no question that respectable and sectarian churches have made life liveable for millions of people, but there is still a big problem for what must be a large majority of the hard living, and it is precisely this question of control. To address it I want to use the metaphor of "game," although I do not mean any disparagement by it. Moreover, it is not language I have heard hard living people use, which is a problem. What I mean by "game" is a set of rules, procedures and practices in a framework of meaning that attempts to order life. The church's game has been one of attempting to order hard living so that it can be under control and not so devastating to the lives of hard living people. This has been especially true in the case of men.

This attempt at control, this game, is perceived in a host of ways by the hard living. It comes through partly in the preoccupation about being "put down" by the church. While there is no question that a basic part of this has to do with demeaning treatment at the hands of church people, it also has to do with the resistance of the hard living to the control of their life-styles which the church represents. Todd said: "The church has a magic, I just don't want it." Jo Ann said that if she went to church and somebody started putting her down, she would just say, "I ain't taking no shit." To be sure, this is resistance to indignities suffered, but it is also the rejection of control.

Sometimes subliminal, sometimes quite forthrightly, the hard living make it clear, not only that they do not buy into the church's game, but that they have a counter-game of their own. Can anyone really doubt that the profane, earthy, sexually explicit, genitally and anally focused, and publicly insensitive four-letter barrage of the hard living is anything if not the attack of a strategy with offense aforethought? When a pastor or lay person meets the hard living in a public or private setting and encounters a language well outside the ritual practices of conventional church life, who has taken the initiative? Who knows how to disrupt whose world? Who understands the ground rules and the tactics of such confrontational engagements? And if the church person moves into the strength of an articulate, "appropriate," conventional discourse aimed at demeaning this "culturally disadvantaged low-life," then the hard living have won again: "the church is full of hypocrites who look down on you, who are uppity, and who think their shit don't stink." It is an extraordinary strategy.

Of course, the response of the hard living is far more complex than I can detail here, even if I understood it all, but the point is that the church's game of control is met with a counter-game of resistance. Once this game and counter-game are in place, it is a beast to break down and build relationships of mutual trust and care. There is no more difficult problem the church confronts in its efforts at evangelization.

Some churches meet this challenge. They are not all of one kind. Indeed, some respectable churches do so by moving out beyond their boundaries, and, of course, the sect-like churches do. Even more importantly, I want to look at a third alternative that addresses this game and counter-game standoff. I talked with the pastors of some forty churches who work with hard living people, where the latter are active members of the congregation. We turn next to the findings of these conversations, and a report on the effective ministries of these churches.

WHAT TO DO

Bill Robinson, the pastor of a church in Little Rock that has a significant ministry with the hard living, was making the point about the necessity of worship reflecting the lives of the people. He said, *"Saturday night and Sunday morning have to come together."* In their service of worship they use musical instruments such as the sax, bass, and drums. "You have to get things people can relate to." He then offered the view that "high church worship does not connect with hard living people."

John Auer, another pastor in Chicago, spoke of a shift in his church from being "open" to being "in solidarity" with hard living people, the necessity of "identification with them." At one time, Auer observed, his church was "open" to the hard living, but "we just didn't go out to them." He reported that they had a kind of "acceptance" of people, a receptivity to their coming, but that was not enough.

"Solidarity goes well beyond openness. It means that a church truly *is* multicultural and multiclass." Their programs, murals on the walls, fellowship dinners, an active small group life, a drop-in center, advocacy, organizing: All of these seek "to give off what they give out."

THE ISSUE OF CONTROL

In Part One I address the issue of control and the fact that the approaches of traditional churches—both conventional, re-

spectable mainline congregations and the sectarian, fundamentalist, Pentecostal ones—tend to operate from a strategy of
control, an attempt to provide a structure or order to replace
the chaos of hard living. While this approach works with some
hard living people, it does not work with many. In fact, the
overwhelming majority of them will at best hustle such
attempts when they need something from such a program, or
they will avoid them altogether. When the churches use such a
strategy—I used the metaphor of a game—it sets up a
counter-control strategy or game on the part of the hard living.
When this strategy/counter strategy gets in place, it becomes a
deadlock, a counter-productive stalemate that is virtually
impervious to missional, outreach, and evangelization efforts
by the church.

From the outset in Part Two, I address this issue, which I
regard as the most basic challenge we have in ministry with the
hard living. Every pastor with the hard living immediately
recognizes this issue and assures me that it is quite real. In our
conversations I find these pastors to have a broad range of
responses to the issue. Their suggestions are quite rich. My
frustration is not that I gain no insight, but rather how
inadequate I feel to convey the wealth of experience and the
down-on-the-ground "truck knowledge" they possessed.* So
long as you understand that what follows is not adequate to
their wisdom I will attempt to convey what I learned.

SETTING THE CLIMATE

A number of things that were offered by these pastors
involved "setting the tone" or "atmosphere" or "getting off on
the right foot." I do not mean their basic theological
orientation or faith stance, although the things to be discussed

---

*"Truck knowledge" is that wonderful range of experience and intimate
acquaintance with something that, if one were hit by a truck, it would be lost. It
is the special understanding one has because of one's unique position in the
world. I learned this notion for the first time from Lovett H. Weems, Jr.

here certainly have profound theological implications. Here the concern is more with a kind of practical wisdom about how a congregation and its pastor establishes an alternative to the control/counter control strategy.

Perhaps the first thing that can be said is that these pastors had an empathic grasp of the relationships that the hard living have had to institutions throughout most of their lives. That is, the hard living expect that institutions do things *to* them, not *for* them and certainly not *with* them. The hard living have had many people do things *to* them: their parents, the schools, employers, the police, the courts, the jails, the welfare system, the government, community service agencies, and, of course, the church.

The hard living also have not had institutions do things *for* them, which sounds strange, I suppose, but it *is* true. While they have been recipients of money and services, so often it is experienced as a form of control or as a way of people "getting rid of them" or as so enveloped in qualifications, rules, and procedures as to be experienced as external and alienating, and then not as something done *with* them. Savvy hard living pastors are acutely sensitive to this history of relationships and attempt to work differently.

Second, and not unrelated to the first, Bonnie Rosen-Cowherd contended that church people must recognize that, as long as we believe that we are the givers and they are the receivers, we will continue to operate out of a control strategy. "We must discover what *we* need, that *we* share, that the hard living have much to give to us." She explained that we must not "put ourselves one up." Bonnie talked especially of the ways in which her understanding of the gospel had "expanded" because of her work with hard living people. "Sometimes our sense of the gospel is nowhere near what the people know who've been to hell and back." While addressing this matter Bonnie also added that everyone needs to know that one's own personal story is important. Sharing makes this possible. "As long as people believe their story does not count," she explained, "they lose power and we lose their contribution."

Third, another important observation surrounded the question of honesty with the hard living. This gave rise to many suggestions: "Don't lie." "Don't make promises you can't keep." "Admit your mistakes." The pastors know that the hard living can recognize dishonesty in an instant. "They know immediately when you are not being truthful, or at least not telling them what's really going on. They know a phony almost immediately."

Fourth, one found much realism among the pastors. Ron Roberts: "We worry too much about getting hustled. It is just going to happen. I get weary of people who attempt to develop a system of delivery of food and clothing that is hustle proof. You can't do it. It's just no contest. They will outwit you every time." He went on: "When people try to close loopholes, they create a façade. They build a lot of hurdles. Then you can't tell the church from the bureaucratic welfare system."

It is not that the pastors want to be hustled; they recognize the need for rules, for policy, and for guidelines. Bernard Keels told me that when the hard living hustle churches, they call it "getting over." This means that "they know how to play the sympathy of the church. You see, they know that the church wants to get rid of them, that the church really does not want them. So they play up to the church sympathy to get the crack money or whatever they need." Bernie told the story of a woman who came to his church to raise money to bury her child. At his spouse's suggestion Bernie decided to call the funeral home to check out the story. There was no child, dead or alive.

Bernie was clear: The church must not give money to people to get rid of them. Instead, the church must become "street-wise and street-smart. We are called to serve, not to be stepped on. Yet, still, we can confront them in a loving way. It is important to tell them we care about them, but that we will not be used by them. We can demand respect without bullying people. I just tell them, 'This is not a get-over place.' But, just as we will not let them 'get-over' us, we will not 'get-over' them.''

There were, of course, many other things that were suggested, but these seem to be the key ones around setting the tone for the ministry. Most of the pastors, however, spoke more directly about developing responses to hard living people that were indigenous to their lives.

6

HARD LIVING MINISTRY

One church in the Midwest discovered a group of hard living people who were living under a bridge in the dead of winter. A compassionate pastor checked with his congregation to see if they could open their inadequate facilities to these people. The church had one shower and a small space where they could sleep. Even so, the church invited them to come. The congregation, actively interested, began working to provide services to these hard living bridge dwellers.

Things went well said the pastor until the church made two requirements: No drugs or alcohol, and no profanity. With that, the men said "No thank you," and left never to return again. They went back to the bridge in freezing weather. Later the church tried a shelter for Mexican-American men, but that failed too. The men would not come. "Maybe they thought there was some arrogance on the part of the church or myself. I don't know. I had been a successful pastor with immigrants, but not with the hard living. It requires a lot of time and commitment. So now I don't try so hard anymore. We may work with someone now and then, but only as an individual."

Why this church failed, I could not clearly say. It was not fully apparent in the interview except that the utterly necessary rapport and relationships never occurred. The pastor told me that "they said they just wanted the free lunch." It is not easy to work with the hard living people, and anyone who begins such a ministry needs to understand as much as possible what one is starting.

This chapter takes a look at pastors and their churches who have done effective work, but it is not so much about programmatic success as it is about the basic orientation of the church and its pastor.

The crucial ingredient is setting the right tone, and what it means to do indigenous ministry. As suggested above the issue of control is central to all these concerns.

RELATIONSHIPS NOT GIMMICKS

The pastors of hard living churches tend to have vigorous opinions about the kind of orientation or approach or style—they use a variety of phrases to express the concern—that a church, its people, and pastor bring to the work. I found their opinions and their concerns unusually helpful and on the mark. In my interviews I would on occasion become too preoccupied with the *how* questions: *How* does one find effective programs? One day when I was especially over-wrought with such queries, Sam Mann, a white Alabaman who has served in an inner-city, African American congregation for two decades, straightened me out.

"It's the wrong question, Tex. You can't do this with gimmicks. You can't gimmick people in. You got to deal with survival and with everyday life. Worship is not dissociated from living. It grows *out* of it, out of survival. *You have to deal with the authenticity of their everyday life.*"

Later, he said that "these are not people we seek to *become* the church. They *are* the church. They *are* Jesus. They are the least of these. They are just what Matthew 25 says."

Sam went on to explain that the key is relationship, but that too many people build programs and promote through gimmicks, and try to do their work around a functional style of talk. All of this is no good, he argued. "You can't build relationships on style, you build them on involvement and being." For Mann the key ingredient is not the *function* or *form* of the ministry but the *quality* of the relationship, a relationship that he sees deeply grounded in a mystical sense of hard living people being the embodied presence of Jesus in the community.

Sam then described the three-pronged focus of the ministry of St. Mark's Church. The first is that of *survival*. He pointed out that the church *must* deal with the issues of food, clothing, jobs, medical care, transportation, housing, whatever. The church "either has to do it or refer people" to agencies that can. *"It is not just something you do. It is essential. It has to be done.* We feed 800 meals a day out of here. We feed the whole neighborhood."

The second prong of ministry is the prophetic emphasis. *"We have to deal with the issues.* The prophetic voice becomes a judgment on the system, that sees the system as victimization in terms of racism, classism, and sexism. The prophetic is problematic for a lot of people, *but here it's part of the job description."* He claims that it's out of the prophetic that "a sense of hope arises."

The third prong is "the vision of a new city." Sam sees this arising from the tension between survival and the prophetic voice. He argues that anyone who has to struggle "knows these things ain't right," and that "the prophetic proclaims the hope." This vision, however, is not mere reform, rather it is transformational. It looks to a new vision, a new city, a transformed urban reality.

LOVE

Chad Burkhardt, the pastor of a Free Will Baptist Church in Indiana, has a warm, evangelical heart and has had a ministry to hard living people for thirty-eight years. In describing his ministry he said, "I'm not a good denominational person. I'm not hung up on being a Baptist. Oh, I tell people I'm Baptist, but I'm just glad Christ got a hold of me before the Baptists did." When asked about his approach, he said, "We've just tried to love 'em to death."

One pastor said, "you have to get in the trenches with them." Another talked about the necessity of "a street orientation." Often sincerity, compassion, and understanding were mentioned. Al Lewis, a pastor in Birmingham, was a former marijuana addict himself, and he felt this "enabled" him to do ministry. *One has "to believe that Jesus meets us where we are*, that Jesus gets in the gutter with us. *Discipleship means meeting people where they are and being with them all the way, it's a process.* It's the building of a life-long relationship."

It is a ministry of "presence" many said. Nancy Kaye Skinner, who has pastored two churches where hard living people were active members, maintained that "the key was the people in the congregation who embraced them and cared about them inside and outside the church." Ron Roberts, a Presbyterian pastor who worked with hard living people for more than twenty-five years commented that there must be a very basic acceptance: "One of the things was very simply that I found these people enormously interesting, sometimes charming, and occasionally heroic." While granting that it could sometimes be quite trying to work with the hard living, he said that you must realize "that most people are doing the best they can." Craig Hunter's comment was close to this when he said, "You have to understand that everybody has a hard time."

Marti Scott served a three-point urban charge in Chicago for twelve years. When I asked her what the most effective programs were, she too turned to a matter that was not programmatic, but spoke significantly to the issue of ministry. Using the word in a way quite differently than Sam Mann had, she said the key factor for her was a matter of *style*. She clearly did not mean a gimmick. Rather she meant something that struck me as deeply incarnational. "It helped that I came from a similar [hard living] background. My style was not to use a title and not to dress like a cleric. I only wore a robe for weddings and funerals." She earned a Ph.D. in historical theology, so she reported that she had to unlearn her theological jargon.

In her preaching she focused on the gospel story and the Old Testament story. She found that "Paul's letters were too judgmental and too conceptual" for the people of her parish. By using stories from the lives of the people themselves she got out from behind the pulpit and stood down on the floor to preach. These and other comments revealed an approach to ministry that was indigenous and formed of the lives and circumstances of the people she served.

"Find a hurt and heal it; find a need and fill it." This has been an important principle in ministry in a variety of contexts for a number of years now. I was struck, however, by a comment Marti Scott made that, upon further reflection, seemed especially indigenous. In discussing this issue of control Marti said that "a sweeping change for me" was an article about professionalism by John McKnight at Northwestern University. He had said that the problem with the social service sector is that we go out and ask what people's *needs* are. McKnight suggested that instead we focus on people's *capacities*. Such reorientation significantly changed the shape of her ministry. She added that people will come to church when they know they are going to be empowered there. A refocusing around people's capacities is a major first step in such empowerment.

Most of the pastors observe that the hard living themselves make the best staff people. Several indicated that they do not have to learn the life-styles, that they really do understand the people, that they are more hustle proof and can recognize genuine concerns from phony ones, and that, when paid, the new staff positions bring more jobs to the community. Hard living people in such staff positions not only utilize their capacities but demonstrate them to the wider community. Using the capacities of hard living people is crucial to indigenous ministry.

Closely related to this idea is that of observing the practices of the hard living to discover what they do effectively in their own lives. Bonnie Rosen-Cowherd and Stuart Whitney spoke of learning from "street action" about how to do teaching and training. After noting the practices that seem to be pervasive on the street, they bring these into the work of the shelter.

Both of them observe the interrelatedness of protection and sharing on the street. The hard living especially attempt to protect and share with newcomers. With many of them these are highly developed street skills. Stuart is interested in both the sharing and protection that occurred around food. "You can't underestimate the power of sharing bread. I had never understood fully how powerful food is. To watch people who have no power share food. Or, to see how important cigarettes and quarters are and how they get shared." Such practices are forms of protection that get worked out between people. Stuart added, "they provide information, help people make it on the street, and tell them where the shelters are. A lot of street action is teaching and training."

With respect to the street practice of sharing, Bonnie has made this a formative aspect of the Wednesday evening worship service at the shelter. "Many of the hard living who come there," she relates, "have a history of going to church and, in effect, saying to the minister or, to the choir or whomever, 'You turn on my switch.' " To change this, Bonnie brings the street practice of sharing into a central place in the worship so that the liturgy really was the work of the people. "At each service we focus on a theme, like forgiveness, then people in the congregation share what it felt like to be or not be forgiven, to forgive or not to forgive. This is then followed with a prayer time, when people ask for very specific prayers." Bonnie says: "They are now sharing the word and 'having church' themselves. This establishes trust. They're doing worship for each other and developing a sense of community."

This is related to a third street practice of *listening*. Bonnie pointed out that hard living people "know how to listen without having to fix it." More than that, "they will listen to the same story over and over again because they know the person needs to be heard." Picking up on this practice Stuart corrects a problem that professionals tend to have: "We need to be careful about the perception that we always have to have the answer. The hard living know that there are no answers to some things."

Pat Morris was a street person for twenty-seven years, a madam for fifteen and a confidence woman for twelve. She has been to prison twice and got out for the last time in 1972 when she became affiliated with the church. She is now a United Methodist pastor. She makes the case, as many do, about how important it is to do ministry "one-on-one" and "to actively and reflectively *listen*." She explains that hard living people "are not often heard. They need a place where they can come and dump. After they've unloaded it all I say, in effect, 'Okay, can you go home now and live for a couple of weeks?' And that's what they do. I don't give advice. I help catharsis and reflect back to them and then ask if I heard right."

I am also struck by a story Stuart Whitney told about a man who had gone through an extremely difficult divorce and a barren loneliness. Stuart asked him about the church, because the man had been a church member. He responded, "listen, the last place where I wanted to talk about my divorce was the church. All they know how to do is celebrate success." I knew exactly what he meant. Respectability is so powerful in the church, that people will not talk about their failures, their weaknesses, their emptiness and loneliness, their inadequacies, and the sheer ragged edges of their lives. But on the street it is different. One cannot hide some things, and the failure and the bad times come with the territory. I do not mean to suggest that hard living people have no pretensions or "play no games." They certainly do. Rather, it is simply not possible to argue credibly that one has it made and that one's life is going swimmingly when you are poor and without residence, a job, or food. In this context "telling your troubles" is basic to the ecology of the life. A church that provides no place for such a practice is simply out of touch with that world.

Does this mean the church should celebrate failure or misery? I do not know, but I can report an interesting experience in a Pentecostal church while doing research on this book. The pastor asked the congregation to think for a moment about the truly bad things that had happened to them in their lives. After they had a moment to do so, he then suggested that they give thanks to God for everything they had endured. And, then, he shouted, "Praise God. Give God the thanks and the glory." I was surprised by the sudden shouts of praise and the gratitude that pattered around me like a soft rain. I remember asking myself what was going on? It seemed to be so important. It seemed *to help*. What did it mean? I called up George Westlake, the pastor of the church, several weeks later. He answered with James 1:2: "Count it all joy. . . . when you meet various trials, for you know that the testing of your faith produces steadfastness." Maintaining that God has a plan for us all, George believes that we can see our hardship as the way God tests us so that we can build our faith. Calling attention to the Greek word for *testing*, he pointed out that it was not the word for temptation but rather for the kind of trial that helps us spiritually mature. "Faith grows more in difficulty than when the time is going easy," he said.

What seems clear here is that it is not so much a celebration of failure as gratitude to God that we are tested and that anything can be turned into an occasion for growth and new life. Furthermore, this approach makes it all right to share the struggless, to be open about the troubled nights of the soul. While it can place any problem, even death, within the wider mercy of God's providence, as we have seen before, it can also give people permission to talk about the down-side of their lives. It is because no event exhausts God's capacity to work with it that such believers can describe the valley of the shadow rather than be constrained by celebrations of success and their affectations.

I believe that the self only emerges in social process and that without such we simply would not be human beings. To say it another way, we are greatly constituted by the everyday lived relationships and practices of our lives as these are constructed and communicated in language. Our relationships, practices, and language are not like some garment that a more substantive part of ourselves takes on and off to be worn or discarded as fits our deeper whims. Rather these are as constitutive of our lives as anything we know or, likely, can know. Such an interpretation means that there can be no form of authentic ministry that is not in some sense indigenous. If that ministry is external, it simply is not a part of our world. Moreover, when it comes to an issue like control, an external form of ministry is worse than unreal, especially when it offers something a person desperately needs, like food or shelter. It then becomes colonial and imperialistic. It is external, imposed, and oppressive, hardly the characteristics of a redemptive and liberative good news. In this sense, indigenous ministry is not a nice additive to an otherwise substantive offering, like paprika on a macaroni salad. Apart from indigeneity in an absolute sense, there is no ministry at all. In more relative terms a ministry that lacks substantive indigeneity is an abstraction, activity and sound cycling and sparking on each other but manifesting the vague and strange unreality of electric signs in pool halls and saloons. No wonder that the hard living reject such ephemeral ministries and all the more so when they exact control.

When these ministries, however, become populated with the practices that grow from the coping and survival rituals that populate the world of the hard living, then the ministry is not alien. It takes on the reality of life as it is in the street. The ministry is no longer the plaything hobby of would-be saviors but rather the hard-earned drills of long-studied survival.

Such indigenous ministry is not, of course, one that simply affirms or attempts to carry out all the practices of hard living. Some of those are clearly destructive and unfaithful, and no one knows it more clearly than the hard living themselves. More than that, they expect the church in some important ways to be in tension with hard living. Any number of the pastors, for example, told me that they were expected to be different and to "walk the talk" of the Christian faith. Otherwise the pastor turned out to be just one more example of the hypocrisy of the church.

In addition, there is a certain kind of almost "magical" belief about a religious leader. Truly devoted religious leaders have "access" to God. God listens to them. They have "influence." If the pastor is not, then, different, he or she cannot be finally effective or of any real help with the Deity. A genuine person of God carries respect and power for hard living people.

CONFRONTATION

These comments, however, do not mean that these pastors could not be confrontational. Sam Mann argued that "with some people you tell them to stop what they are doing because you love them." Patricia Meyers stated that she was known as a person "who will talk to anybody, drunks, abusers, you name it, but there are some things I won't give 'em comfort about. One guy came in and I chewed his butt for a half-hour. You see, I talk their language, and I said, 'You really screwed up big time.' " Yet, as confrontive as she was, I could tell Pat had a passionate concern for the well-being of the man she talked to, a fact supported by his continuing to relate to her and to stick with the church. Nelson "Fuzz" Thompson, who has had a long ministry with the children of the hard living, believes that "You've got to be willing to fall out with the kids, because you've got to stand for something. I reject the concept of a drop-in center for children that glorifies nothing. We must not give positive regard to this 'living a slick life.' It's negative to allow kids to hang out. Programs need to be planned, organized, and laid out. There's no pride where there's no discipline."

Even so, as confrontational as they can be, these hard living pastors also know how crucial it is on other kinds of occasions to be supportive and nonjudgmental. Burkhardt said "I never tell a fellow he ought not to drink. He knows that. I just tell him that Christ is the answer and that Christ loves him as much as any other person in the whole world. You see, I came from the same background, so I'm living proof that Christ makes a difference and they know I didn't do it on my own."

Stuart Whitney observed that a lot of hard living people he had known had church backgrounds but no longer attended. When he asked why they fell through the cracks, most say that they did not experience support. "We all need support systems," he said pointedly, "and these people come here without them. We're here to make sure they get it [support]."

DESPERATE PATHOS

I struggle to put more flesh on these approaches, yet, I am so touched by their comments that I often find myself in tears and fighting to keep my voice clear.

The vitality, the humor, the realism, the tested faith, the bruised hope, the capacity to care, the durable courage: These things make the point even more than what they say. Ministry with the hard living is more than the execution of creative ideas or gimmicks or human engineering or high-power administration or keen sociological insight or psychological analysis or a theological tour de force—all of these could be found among these pastors—but it is finally something about *who* they are altogether and about the *way* they are and *Whose* they are. It was never one thing. They inevitably give a damn, they get into the trenches, they like the people, and they are often like the people. They can take a stand, become rock hard when they must, and yet there is a tenderness, sometimes behind a rough exterior, that grows out of the best kind of compassion, the kind that sticks and does not run away when things go wrong. Finally, there is always, *always*, the conviction that God is doing important work in their midst and that they are part of something that is desperately important.

In saying this I do not mean to suggest that these were superhuman people. They are as quick as anyone to own the foibles , the finitude, the failures of their ministries and of their own persons. One pastor confesses that she has been caught up in the dysfunctionality of the setting, another talks of being sick after more than ten years of an exhausting pastorate, one has attempted suicide, all of them talk of the hard times and the despair, but there is *not one* who questioned the importance of the ministry or the reality of God's action in their midst.

Sam Mann is right. It is not a ministry of gimmicks or of rationalized procedures, or technically correct methods. None of these things, taken alone, provides the sustaining basis or the empowering motivation or the vital endurance to live out a faithful ministry among the hard living. Rather the crucial factors are those of faith: of a God moving in the world, of a Christ appearing and reappearing again and again in the lives of the hard living, of a conviction that the church simply cannot be, must not be, an in-grown group made up only of "our kind of people."

I am certain that there are days for these pastors when these towering theological convictions must seem dim and beyond the vision of that immediate problem of some hard living person drunk again, or in jail again, or trying once more to hustle the church, or some "righteous" member trying to protect the building, or save money by avoiding ministry. To be candid, sometimes these pastors seem to speak as much to gird up their own courage as to inform me. On occasion, they seem to be "rehearsing" or "practicing" these claims, a ritualized form of remembering whose they are and why they are there, a liturgy of the work of ministry reminding themselves why they must stay. In these settings there are times where there is little or nothing that one could *see* to offer hope, but these pastors know that one first must believe in order to see anything at all. Seeing is not believing—contrary to my twenty-five years in Missouri—rather to believe is to see. And their believing makes the vision possible. They believe Christ is in their midst and through such faithfulness they see messianic work in hard living and sense a redemptive current moving in their communities. There is finally no substitute for such discernment and no other source of strength for those caught in a world of despair where the hunger runs so deep for the reality of legitimate hope.

7

COMFORTABLE PREACHING AND WORSHIP

I sat down in the sanctuary about two-thirds of the way back in a crowd of about six hundred people at a Pentecostal service in a church in Kansas City. Up front, a piano, bass, drums, and saxophone were doing a fast-paced contemporary gospel song, all of them electrified except for the drums. The congregation moved to the music, some raising hands in prayer, others patting their feet , a good many praying quietly in tongues, and occasionally someone shouted "Praise the Lord!" The crowd had an impressive mixture of African-Americans, Hispanics, Asians, a few Native Americans, and Anglos (with the last in the majority, but not greatly so). It was the most "integrated" church service I had been to since the Martin Luther King, Jr. celebration. If I can "read class," my "guesstimate" was that about fifty percent were lower-middle to middle class, about thirty percent working people, and easily twenty percent were into or not far removed from hard living. In front of me two rows up and two seats over were two bikers with big Harley Davidson patches on the backs of their jean jackets and several smaller ones on the front that I couldn't read.

I was green with envy. I could not remember the last time I had seen bikers in a mainline church, or this kind of integrated service, or the presence of so many people who were clearly poor or nearly so. Then I got angry, deep-down raw angry, at the homogeneity principle frothed about in the land today by church "experts" and pastors and lay people who observe that we work best with "our own kind of people."

I was not at the Glide Church in San Francisco or some other well-known, highly endowed program that had a nationally known pastor, or was exceptional. I mean no disparagement by this comment since I am enormously grateful for churches like Glide, but my focus in this book is about what more "ordinary" churches can do, who can perform vital ministry with the hard living even without large resources. It was merely a big Kansas City Pentecostal church that served the lower end of the class structure. It was not in a good location, and its building looked more like a gymnasium than an ecclesiastical edifice. Such thoughts only upset me more.

I was, therefore, glad when it came time to sing the first "hymn." When I looked, I could not find my hymnal, and then I discovered that the "bulletin" was not an order of worship at all, but a leaflet announcing and describing a host of ministries the church offered for the coming week with a few events that were scheduled beyond that. By now I realized that the "hymn" was a "praise song" and that the words were being flashed via a transparency projector onto the large white wall behind the platform. The words, however, were simple, easy to learn, and by the time one came to the chorus a second time, they were well in mind.

Meanwhile, one Hispanic young man had taken a microphone, backed up by six other singers similarly equipped, and was leading the crowd through several rousing, vigorous praise songs, one right after the other. I was singing as boisterously as I could while enjoying the full sound that permeated the room and drowned out my mistakes without diminishing my fervor. It was the second or third praise song before I realized that some people were hardly singing and others not at all. To be sure most were, and a good many as loud as I, but what was significant was that it did not matter. I was struck that such an arrangement overcame the problem of people who sing in church as if they had strep throat. Such oppressive lethargy had no chance here.

As the service moved on I became aware that one did not have to read or even be literate to be an active part of that service. When I looked more carefully I could see that some paid no attention to the bulletin or the transparency projections. My impression was that some of them were functionally illiterate, and I was touched by the fact that such things formed no barrier here. Had I not been so moved I would have been upset again by church services where one balances a printed bulletin, selected worship resources, and hymns with five verses and no chorus, which one encounters steadily in literate liturgies.

Later there was a testimony in tongues which was promptly interpreted by a reading from Scripture. The pastoral prayer was accompanied by quiet glossolalia, raised hands, and punctuated by "Hallelujah," "Amen," and "Praise the Lord." There was a solo sung with feeling, and a passionate sermon that separated clearly the ways of a lost world and the one way in Jesus Christ. By my count twenty-five people had an up-front participative role in that service. The pastor preached and did the pastoral prayer and benediction. Except for those three things all the rest was done by a number of others, not the least by a highly participative congregation that often shouted a *Yes* or *Amen* in dialogic response.

ORAL WORSHIP

Perhaps this service cannot serve altogether as a model. It has its problems. A pervasive individualism could have completely blotted out the corporate character of the faith had it not been so clearly the gathering of a body and not merely an assembly of individuals. While the pastor spoke against alcohol and related personal issues, he said nothing about the pervasive message of social righteousness in scripture and the prophetic passion for justice. No one said anything about peace except for the subjective kind that occurs in the hearts of individual believers. While I take a choice position on the abortion controversy, I felt myself strangely relieved to discover pro-life materials in the foyer. At least, I said to myself, they express *some* concern for social policy and contemporary issues. Yet, most of all, nothing in that service addressed the substantive injustices that led to the poverty and near-poverty of so many gathered *there* on that very morning.

Nevertheless, one can learn a great deal from the style of that service and not a little from some of its substance. In the interviews with the pastors of hard living churches certain themes clearly appeared in their remarks that were quite evident in that Pentecostal service. If the church is to bring together hard living spirituality and participation in congregational life, then forms of worship which speak directly to the lives of hard living people will be paramount. Such worship will be oral in style, will give music of a certain kind a central place, will provide preaching that is "down on the ground," aimed directly at the day-to-day struggles they face and that speaks assurance and a message of hope. Such worship will be open to opportunities for participative intercessory prayer, testimony, will be informal in style, and receptive to a wide range of dress and clothing. We can turn now to the findings of our conversations with hard living pastors about these matters.

Mainline churches make a major mistake in their ministry with the poor by being too literate and not oral enough. This is especially true in worship. Not only are there large numbers of the poor who are functionally illiterate, but even those who can read and write are more likely to come to or at life in an oral rather than a literate fashion. They are not print oriented. Ron Roberts, for example, said that sometimes he "could count seventeen members in a congregation of sixty or seventy who could not read well because of sight problems, borderline literacy, or retardation. So I went to a nonwritten liturgy. We went to an oral worship. I would ask questions and they would respond. We used the Twenty-third Psalm for an affirmation of faith, which we repeated from memory in unison."

Pat Meyers: "I try not to rely on the bulletin because a lot of people can't read." "When I teach a hymn, I don't do it from the hymnal. I line it out, that is, I sing a line and then have them do it until we work our way through it." Marilyn Gebert: "I started out as a third grade teacher and I stayed basically at the third grade level. I tell stories. I don't use notes [when she preaches], and I go out to the people." Jane White-Stevens: "We tried to use less sophisticated praise songs that were easy to sing, that didn't require a hymnal." Sharon Garfield: "The community is having to teach me. I'm learning. The only way I have tendencies toward being Pentecostal is through my storytelling ability. I'm not terribly abstract anyhow; I don't think theoretically. I'm getting much more personal with my illustrations. I try to show what was going on then and what's going on now. I take a word of hope and try to show people how to take power."

The worship services in the hard living churches are also informal as a rule. Chuck Kallaus describes his approach to worship as "loose, informal, and with a lot of talking back. Prayer was usually offered 'on the spot' when a concern came up. They loved to sing. They weren't interested in liturgy, and they liked short sermons." Sethard Beverly, a national urban executive for the Church of God, Anderson, says that the worship needs to be celebrative, free and not locked into order and form.

These informal services typically involve much movement on the part of the congregants. John Auer points out how important it is to get people involved physically, such as tying a prayer on a Jesse tree or passing the peace, "which can get started and be difficult to stop." John also took pews out in the back so that the coffee hour could be held in that space and immediately precede worship with a gathering there. Robert Metheny says that they did away with the altar call in his church, but the hard living still needed "an overt time of commitment on a regular basis. They need a way to affirm publicly and physically that they've made a commitment."

Physical movement during worship is actually one aspect of services that are highly participative. George Miller describes a significant level of lay involvement in the services at his church. Most Sundays "all I do is preach." The laity conduct the service, offer the pastoral prayer every other week, do the children's sermon, and a lay person preaches every ten weeks. Marilyn Gebert describes her sermons as "very dialogical." "If I ask a question they answer it. They talk back to me while I preach." Al Lewis describes his service where people "get up, walk around, share, hug, and make people feel accepted and loved." Kendall Link, formerly a chaplain in a county prison, also reports the profound importance of inmate participation in offering prayer, Scripture reading, and leading the service.

One key part of this participation is testimony, although it is not always called that. Rexine Bryant says that in her church "*sharing* is a good word, and *testimony* is a bad word," but sharing what the gospel has meant to them is an important part of hard living worship. Sharon Garfield tells the story of a worship service at her church early on in her ministry there. She had prepared "a literate worship" and "everything was wrong." When she got to the offering, she made a statement about "the giving of yourself." Nothing happened. The other pastor said nothing, and, finally, Billy Mims, a young Hispanic lay person in the congregation, stood up and told the gathering that he had been fighting the call to go into the ministry, but that he now intended to answer that call. With that, others got up and gave their own testimony. "From then on, it turned around. Nobody wanted to leave. They kept saying 'It's the best service we ever went to since we've been coming to this church.' "

As with Sharon's church, most of the congregations I heard from were multiethnic. The characteristics we have discussed so far seemed to be effective regardless of the ethnicity of the participants, but it is still important to be faithful to these differences and to celebrate the variety of cultures and histories represented in a congregation. John Auer, for example, uses a variety of styles and music in worship: African-American, Asian, Hispanic, Native American, and Anglo. He also reports that they developed a monitoring technique to keep up with how much their worship reflects the different racial groups in the church. Recently, they did special work on Caribbean Americans and made use of their history, culture, and music as part of worship.

Pat Morris uses music, art, puppetry, and mime to address the various ethnics and life-styles in worship. "People's life experience and tradition have to be exhibited so that they can participate fully." Al Lewis adds another dimension to this. Believing that Jesus spoke through the culture of his time and being a professional musician himself, he takes "music off the street" and rewrites the words using the Christian message. He sees himself in the tradition of David writing the *Psalms* or like forebears in the faith who took drinking songs and turned them into faith classics.

FERVENT PRAYER

It is difficult to exaggerate the role of prayer among many hard living people. I remember once being called to the hospital by a friend who was a biker. I had performed the wedding ceremony for him and his spouse, surrounded by thirty-something motorcycles in the middle of the street. A year later on the way home on his motorcycle they were hit broadside by someone "who didn't see them." Now in the hospital with an excruciatingly painful broken hip, that would prove to be permanently crippling, he asked me to come. I wondered all the way there what I would do or say. Should I take on a pastoral role or should I be there only as a friend? Should I offer prayer, for example, or should I simply express my well-wishes? I did not want to impose my religious practices on him, but at the same time I wanted to be a pastor, since I knew he had none, if that was what he wanted. I did not have to worry. When I stepped over the threshold of that hospital room, Ike looked at me with some urgency and said immediately "Oh, Tex, I'm glad you're here. Please come and pray for me." When I walked to his bedside, he reached up, pulled me down to hold him, and asked me to pray. It was a fervent prayer and one made even more urgent by his "Amens" and "Yes Lords."

My experience is not unique according to the hard living pastors. The more personal and directly focused, the better. Jane White-Stevens said "they do not like generic prayers. The requests for prayer were for each need: jobs, sickness, children." Rexine Bryant remarked that "they want prayer by name." She offered that "the purpose of this in worship is to cast your cares on Jesus because he cares for us. We cannot worship if we are burdened down by care." Seth Beverly also pointed out how important it is that prayers during worship be focused on loved ones, illness, and quite specific problems like the drug addiction of a family member.

In this same vein many of the pastors said that prayer time needs to be open and free so that people can voice their own personal petitions to God. These become an important group experience. Pat Meyers told me that the hard living people she worked with had no use for the prayer of confession. "It's stupid," they said. "I haven't done any of those things. A prayer of confession ought to be for what I've done." Nevertheless some printed prayers were used. Pat always printed the Lord's Prayer just in case some didn't know it. Beyond that though, Craig Hunter uses printed prayers but also freedom of expression and, like many of the pastors, provides the opportunity for prayer at the altar, an important practice for some of the hard living.

Sharon Garfield pointed out that even the children ask for prayer. She related the story of one little girl who told the church that her aunt had been shot to death. "She sobbed and sobbed through the service but needed to place it before the congregation."

Prayer is, of course, as important a resource as we have in relationship to God. Among the hard living this takes on express importance because of their views on the immediacy of God's providence. God is involved in the finite details of everyday life in a direct, determinative way. Appeals to God before such a reality make all the sense in the world to the hard living. Furthermore, in a world so often experienced as beyond control this mighty God can take charge and turn the stampede of a hard fate in the direction of healing and a new opportunity. More than this even, hard living people are not usually struggling with an approach to prayer life that fits coherently into a systematic, discursive theology which can withstand the theoretical whipsaws of academic debate—a process that has its own salience and urgency in the wider work of the church. Rather the hard living struggle more with believing than with knowing, with assurance than with explanation, with trust than with doctrine, with hope than with the idea of history, and with a providential God more than with theodicy, although the latter can clearly come into play as we have seen with "the God who fails." But one does not have to deny the importance of what the hard living tend to ignore in order to see the life and death significance of what they affirm. In a church of tender compassion there will be time to bring fuller reflection to such questions as they arise—and they inevitably will—and by this means to draw on an encoded, usually tacit but more fully informed, understanding of a world not so exactly in tune with the good will of a loving God. Hard living people are not impervious to the learnings of an honest spiritual life, their resistance has been far more deeply formed by the self-righteous bearings of a demeaning church.

COMMON MUSIC

We have already heard from Bill Robinson in terms of how he attempts to bring Saturday night to Sunday morning in the music of his church and from Al Lewis who takes street music and rewrites the words. Jane White-Stevens uses contemporary music, praise hymns, and Christian radio songs. Staying away from "sophisticated music" she employs material that is "easy to sing." Craig Hunter offers a variety of music, but the gospel choir which was racially mixed, was most well received with its Black Gospel sound, although a majority of the group was Anglo. Along with many others Rexine Bryant scheduled sing-a-longs, where the congregants picked the hymns, but she also occasionally taught a new hymn as well. Gene Liddick gave a central place to children in worship and found that the hard living parents would usually come to hear their youngsters sing. Cleo Coleman said that "gospel numbers" were the best received music in her church, and that African Americans, whites, and, for the most part, the Hispanics liked this same music. Kendall Link found that old gospel songs were the most appreciated in the county prison as well. A structured approach was suggested by Patricia Meyers. While the first hymn is an old one, the hymn of preparation is usually a new one, a contemporary hymn, which she teaches in oral fashion by lining it out. The last hymn is a "Fanny Crosby, evangelistic hymn," like "Leaning on the Everlasting Arms" or "Beulah Land." All of the pastors report that their hard living members love to sing and that music is key in their worship.

Several of the pastors informed me that they had difficulty with organists and choir directors who were quite resistant to playing or singing music that was not "good" or "traditional" or "classical." Bach, Beethoven, Brahms, and Mozart were typically the staple of these musicians, and they seemed to see their vocation as that of "lifting" the musical tastes of the congregation. A few of these were purists who felt "compromised" by participating in the musical "debauchery" of contemporary, gospel, African American, and country-western music. In too few instances these musicians were terminated.

As a consultant to congregations around the country I have found any number of churches cowed by such musicians who continue to perform—and *perform* is the right word—for congregations where the overwhelming majority of people do not find their mono-type and elitist selections spiritually nourishing; indeed, they find them dull and boring. Such instrumentalists and singers apparently see themselves making music upon some Archimedean stage foundationed on universal musical tastes which they broadcast to a backward, ignorant and recalcitrant audience. If such musicians will not hear the concerned urgings of appropriate committees and officials, they should be lovingly fired. A faithful indigenous worship cannot afford the sociohistorical parochialism of people who believe universality of musical taste emerges from the last several hundred years among elites in Western Europe and the United States. And pastors with similar "standards" need reassignment to status churches in some university towns where the congregations enjoy the stuffy hegemony of delayed musical schools who have not yet looked beneath the assumptions of their "universalities" to discover that no known foundation is there.

ANOINTED PREACHING

Good preaching with the hard living takes on a number of clear characteristics according to the pastors we interviewed. For one thing Cleo Coleman said it has to be fervent, a note sounded also by Seth Beverly. Richard Mark offered a second characteristic that preaching needs to be "nonjudgmental, uplifting, not vindictive, and inspirational." As he spoke I immediately remembered the hard living people who would not go to a church where the preacher "hollered at you" and "put you down." Another important instruction came from Jane White-Stevens which was stated by others, to wit, that preaching has to be "biblically centered," but based on "common life experiences." Jane found the focus of the twelve-step program of Alcoholics Anonymous very helpful. People with A.A. backgrounds came and heard her speaking their language, and the concepts of A.A. were "so relevant that they worked for everybody." The notion of facing "one day at a time," for example, spoke to many, as did ideas of giving oneself over to a higher power, taking a moral inventory of oneself, making amends to persons one had wronged, and so on. As a result the word got out among the hard living that this was someone who spoke their language and understood. Marilyn Gebert also dealt quite concretely with issues before the people in her congregation: alcohol and drugs, child abuse, how to get through the week, and hope, "a lot about hope." Nelson Thompson agreed that you *must* preach hope; "it's all some people have." Along these same lines Kendall Link discovered in his preaching in the county prison that the Lazarus theme and the resurrection theme struck home. He said, "the idea that you don't have to stay the way you are, the idea that the stone will be rolled away and they can step out into new life. . . . Even with lifers, these themes became at least a spiritual freedom. A lifer could be standing behind bars, but through the bars he could hold the dove of peace." Finally, several mentioned that preaching needs to be informal. The pastor should move around, that one should never read from a manuscript and—perhaps the hope of laity everywhere—that the sermon should not be too long.

   In talking with the forty pastors about worship I was struck by how intentional they were to make worship a "comfortable" experience, to use a word advanced by one of the hard living in Part One. A "comfortable church" provides full participation in worship through song, sharing, testimony, prayer, and even in their "dialogic" relationship to preaching. They had leadership responsibilities, and the style and content of these services were quite explicitly designed to include them in, to make them feel at home, and to experience oral and liturgical forms that spoke in and through their lives. At this point, perhaps, just two things can be lifted up. The first is that in a world of separation, abandonment, alienation, and demeaned worth we need to realize what it means to find a church where one is *at home*, that speaks one's language, that offers opportunity for expression consistent with the practices of one's everyday life, and that names the problems and struggles one battles with in a context of hope. Such indigenous hospitality proclaims the good news in a way that cannot be reduced to any one part of a service. For people who feel they have no home, it is an ecological kerygma, an environmental proclamation of their worth to God, of their acceptance in Christ, and of their ties to others in the community of faith. There is finally no substitute for this.

Secondly, it is devastating to contemplate the opposite. If one cannot read, what is proclaimed in a church where the central act of worship requires literacy? Or, even if one can read and write but is still basically oral in one's approach to life, what is the message of a church steeped in literate expression? I think it says the gospel is not for those who are different. Surely, if anything is an abomination, an abhorrent, detestable, loathing to God, this is one of the foremost.

8

NONLITERATE
CHRISTIAN EDUCATION

Christian education takes on special forms with the hard living, but it is a vital part of the ministry of the churches that reach the hard living. Here, too, some of the pastors address the issue in terms of an appropriate orientation or approach. Seth Beverly, for example, maintained that you have to "take people where you find them." He uses an approach that is oral and that focuses on feelings. The hard living also learn by anecdote or story and through discussion. Seth refuses to lecture, but instead he likes "to get it going" and then "to guide the discussion." It is helpful, he points out, to affirm what people say in such conversations, and the use of video is especially appropriate with people who are raised on T.V.

Seth also contends that Christian education with the hard living must be life-centered. One cannot merely promulgate doctrine. "We need to be teaching people how to clean up, learn job skills, and to cope in the business and commercial world. If the teaching does not get down on the ground, it won't work."

In his own teaching Seth uses few books because he finds brief articles much more helpful. He attempts to compress ideas from books and articles so that he can get those before people for discussion where they can be picked apart and can generate lively disagreement. With the short attention spans that many have, he finds this method to be much more productive. Al Lewis proposes that we teach a relevant gospel, one that both indicates and demonstrates "that God is for you and sent his Son for you." In his work he proclaims that "we are an overcoming people." "We all struggle," he says, "but that's true of every biblical character also. I try to say to them that God will be with you and God will deliver you."

"But I don't preach a prosperity gospel," says Al as he clarifies, "because it is corruptive. We should not emphasize a prosperity gospel because our prosperity is in an internal, spiritual prosperity. God can give you peace even in a storm. A relevant gospel points not to things but to God." One should not conclude from this, however, that Al is not concerned about the material lives of his people. A broad range of ministries takes their physical and spiritual needs with the utmost seriousness. He also "teaches his people from the cultures of Africa. We need these things to learn self-esteem."

PROBLEMS

Christian education with the hard living poses special problems. For one thing, they sometimes do not fit in with the more traditional Sunday school schedule. Pat Meyers finds that late-night, heavy drinking usually goes on Saturday evening, and it's almost impossible to get them out by 9:30 in the morning." So instead they have coffee and conversation at 10:30, before worship. This is quite popular, she says, and encourages people at least to make the 11:00 service. "They just bring their coffee right in with them." Difficulty integrating the hard living into other aspects of the education program is an issue as well. "Dress is an issue," says one pastor. "The middle class wears suits and ties, and the hard living jeans." But "group life" is an issue too. The hard living in his church want to be mainstreamed, but cleanliness becomes a problem here as well. For example, different standards in the preparation of food for church suppers has led to stomach sickness on occasion. Other problems pop up around spiritual traditions. The hard living often have a more Pentecostal background, report some pastors, and, as one said, "they've had a tough time with the structure of our church."

So it is not always easy. Differences in style, in standards of dress and hygiene, and decorum must constantly be managed. Sometimes the structure of traditional church life is out of phase with hard living practices, and, of course, some things just do not work.

BIBLE STUDY

If anything receives universal comment by the pastors in terms of its effectiveness in Christian education, it is Bible study. Marti Scott: "The Scriptures were extremely important. They took them with great seriousness, and any occasion to teach about the Bible brought active participation by the hard living." One group, for example, "took on the Jubilee and really ran with it." Jane White-Stevens agreed with Marti about the central importance of Scripture. "They want the Bible, and they trust it. It is their main spirituality. They trust the Bible, and they trust A.A. Seth Beverly pointed out that they were not interested in the academic study of the Bible. In fact, in most any kind of study, Seth said, "the more academic, the more reading, the less they are interested."

The basic interest according to Bob Metheny has to do with the implications of Bible study for their daily lives. A number of pastors in talking about Bible study note, as Marti Scott does earlier, that biblical stories are more helpful than conceptually developed writing like that of Paul's. In this connection Bob Metheny says that Bible study "needs to be unambiguous." "It needs to be clear, authoritative, and simple." Bob explains that Bible study must not "undermine where they come from. They have too much ambiguity in their lives already. They have enough problems. They do not need any more. They need to deal with the implications for what it means in their concrete experience."

I can understand, of course, why many pastors would be troubled by Bible study that refuses ambiguity, yet one can certainly see the point Bob is making about the mixed uncertainties of hard living lives. This is one place where I think we can trust, over the long haul, the tacit wisdom and understanding that hard living people have. By honing in on real issues in their lives the complexities will emerge in settings where they find acceptance and trust. They know, at least most of them, that the world is uneven at best and that there really are not simple answers to the heaviest problems that life brings. If their use of language does not satisfy discursive coherence, the constellation of rips and tears in the coarse fabric of their existence will be finally more telling than the silky smooth talk of easy certainties. In my experience the absolutes of hard living affirmations have much more to do with trust and assurance and the search for loyalty than with assertions of lobotomized clarity aimed at an absolute filtering of the exceptions. Hard living is filled with exceptions. I think one can finally trust that.

Bob works with the Disciple Bible Study program and finds this to be effective. It combines prayer and study of the Scriptures. He reports, however, that the hard living can get wild with interpretation. With a strong Pentecostal contingent in his group, he says that they can be chaotic and, thus, need the structure the Disciple study provides.

Pat Meyers, however, had a different view. She complained about the lack of materials aimed at their reading level. "I'm dealing with fourth and fifth grade reading levels. We have had to look at David C. Cook. We take their curriculum and then re-do it. We did the Disciple Bible Study, but not with the hard living. It was too advanced. People in the area around my church are deeply influenced by Fundamentalism. They are surrounded by this stuff about a vengeful, judgmental God. What we [mainstream pastors] poke fun at is alive and well on the street, for example, a young woman recently said to me, 'my baby just died, and God is punishing me.' I'm constantly battling this stuff."

If Bob Metheny has been able to use Disciple Bible Study and Pat Meyers has not, I suspect they do agree on another point made by Bob. As a United Methodist he argues that "we can't give up on who we are. We need to talk about our own tradition of assurance and sanctification. We need for them to be who they are, but in our context." Any church sensitive to the importance of its traditions would make this claim. There are substantive affirmations and identities that one can be faithful to and still be open to forms of ministry—oral, expressive, participative, testimonial—which are indigenous to hard living. In speaking out of my own United Methodist moorings I have maintained that in working with the poor one can be Pentecostal in style and Wesleyan in substance. While the boundary between form and substance can be quite thin in some instances, this has not been a major issue in my conversations with hard living pastors.

This question of identity may be important in other respects as well. Jane White-Stevens finds, also, that Bible study in small groups is well attended by the hard living. In her experience the hard living like a Bible study where they talk very honestly. "Generally, they focus on themselves." She discovers that "alcoholics sometimes seem like teenagers. In their cycle of meeting needs, if you don't meet identity needs, then you can't go into intimacy. They first had to deal with identity." This is an important psychological point, but I suspect it is also an important theological point, one where the identity of the church itself, whatever modification it makes in form of ministry, is important in meeting the spiritual and community needs of the hard living. Jane finds that when the hard living got beyond these identity questions, "they threw themselves into ministry." One man who spent several years in a mental hospital, later committed himself to visiting jails and nursing homes. One couple went to work for an urban center; others were reaching out to people who were down-

and-out. Jane reports what many others have observed that the hard living are very willing to be in service to others in behalf of the church.

CHILDREN AND YOUTH

Many of the pastors find that the Sunday school, though important, was not adequate in reaching the children and youth of the hard living. Those who come are usually sent and not brought, and participation on Sunday morning is simply not adequate. With the children three programs seem to be especially good. One of these was an after-school program organized like a Vacation Bible School, but that meets once a week. The second is like the first except it occurs in the early evening. These programs often draw fifty to a hundred children and are able to reach diversities of ethnic groups: African American, Hispanics, Asians, and Anglos. The children from hard living families especially enjoy these sessions and would come when they did not attend Sunday school. A third program is a summer day camp. David Boyd has a program like this in his church. It offers the opportunity for the children to visit a wide variety of places all across the metropolitan area and is well attended.

With respect to the youth Chad Burkhardt said that he has always been oriented to children and youth. "If I can get the children and youth, I can get the parents." He has three programs going on Sunday evening: the young adult, the six to eleven, and twelve-to-eighteen year olds. He relates that his church is youth oriented and that with these age level ministries he is able to draw large numbers of youth on the one hand but also adults to work with them on the other.

Marti Scott attempts to provide "an alternative sense of family" with her youth and children's programs. "A lot of our young people are embarrassed by their families, by their alcohol and drug use, their unemployment and so on." Her church, therefore, attempts to be a family with these children.

In her work she finds values clarification especially helpful with the youth and has attempted to develop the idea of citizenship. She raises questions with young people about "what it means to get a caring sense for the community, for keeping the neighborhood clean, and for watching out for one another."

Consistent with hard living interest in Bible study Marilyn Gebert discovered that the youth have great interest in a Bible Quiz sponsored by her church's district. "The youth really came together around it. We lost the first two times, but won the last three. They were proud because they were able to show those kids in the fancy churches."

A variety of other programs were suggested. Boy Scouts and Girl Scouts work well. David Boyd has a Homework Club, staffed by volunteers that meet a real need for the youth in his church. That same church has a Native American and a Hispanic program that highlights and affirms the ethnicity of their teenagers. Of course, trips are always a favorite with the young people and have been put to a good purpose by a number of the churches in expanding the horizons of the youth about the community and their awareness about the mission and the work of the church. And, finally, Bill Robinson emphasizes that their church stressed spirituality throughout the entire range of their program. "We try to help our young people get in touch with self, with God, and with what's right and wrong." This emphasis extended to a variety of A.A. and other twelve-step programs sponsored by the church, which focused on spirituality as an essential dimension of this effort.

ADULTS

Some of the churches report having a difficult time doing Christian education with hard living adults simply because they will not participate. Other churches, however, find ways to get through and involve the hard living. Rexine Bryant, for example, discovered that her hard living members love to play Scruples, a commercially produced game that places each participant in a situation involving a difficult moral choice. It proved to be an excellent way to bring Scripture into play in such situations and to provide opportunity to think about ethics and its relationship to faith. Rexine also employed biblical charades as a way to combine a playful good time with their interest in Bible study, a pastime her people have used again and again. She explains that she would usually tell or read a Bible story so that the game could be based on the characters in that particular narrative, which gives the participants a more equal footing.

The twelve-step program has shown itself to be crucial in her work, and she has led a lot of the fifth-step groups on confession. A support group for survivors of incest had also met a genuine need among some of her people, and Rexine says that she involved hard living people who were recovering from alcohol and drug abuse in working with Scouts, a practice that has been helpful to them and to the youth. The wonderful creativity like that in Rexine's work and others demonstrates what these compassionate pastors have been able to do when they combine faithful mission and indigenous ministry.

FOUR LEADERSHIP TIPS

The work of these pastors in worship and Christian education is driven by four things. The first is the resourcefulness and creativity they bring to their work when most of them operate on a shoestring. They virtually can do anything with almost nothing. It is a fitting testimony to what can be done when people set out to be faithful to the leading of God's spirit. They indeed do "make a way out of no way." Second, it is striking how committed they are to making the church a place of hospitality for hard living strangers. They do fail at this, and often according to their own reports, but it is hard to believe that their embodied and institutionalized message of acceptance of or commitment to hard living people is utterly squelched even by the suppressive blanketing of poverty and addiction. Third, doubtlessly control issues emerge in the policies and rules of any organization, but these churches, it seems to me, have been as dedicated to alternative ministry in worship and education as they know how to be. The deep involvement of the hard living in the leadership and the direct ministry of the churches whose practices come from concrete hard living lives is perhaps the only way finally to break down the control/counter-control stalemate that separates the two.

Finally, the temptation to demeaning charity is nowhere as great as it is in the provisions of food, clothing, and services to hard living people. We turn to this in the next chapter. Here we shall again face the issue of control, and we must, also, deal more directly with the matter of protest and resistance.

9

PROTEST AND RESISTANCE

Time and again, we have seen how important the issue of control is in ministry with the hard living, but this issue is also deeply related to a dimension of protest and resistance. When these features are not adequately appreciated, the church and other community organizations will not only misunderstand the hard living, they will also miss out on a major resource for change, for advocacy, and for political action in behalf of justice for the poor.

This dimension of protest and resistance can be found in people who tell you early on that "I ain't gonna take no shit," or that "nobody better not fuck with me." It can be seen in the subtle, but pervasive counter-control strategy in response to church efforts to order their circumstances. It is clear that hard living cannot be reduced simply to passivity and self-loss, that failure to see in their actions a protest of the world and of the futility of their situation is to miss the part of them that still bears hope and capacity for change. Even in drug abuse itself one can discern refusal. While I believe that most drug addiction is genetically based, this does not dent the contention that it is also a form of protest. Even if all addiction were genetic or chemically caused, a generalization that would be enormously difficult if not impossible to prove, this would not rule out the claim that it is also the occasion to level a declaration of dissent and of active opposition to the world that the hard living know.

Their protest and resistance are among the basic reasons why authentic ministry must be indigenous and why it can only be faithfully done in identification and in solidarity with them. To do ministry *for* instead of *with* the hard living begins a one-down relationship that triggers a dynamic of opposition. This can take at least two forms. One is covert, especially when the hard living need what the other has. Then the tactics of the powerless are employed with an imaginative creativity that deserves appreciation and awe. They have, says de Certeau a "mobile infinity of tactics." These tactics would make Machiavelli look naive and lacking in subtlety. Theirs is an endless versatility of procedures: Testing the rules, limiting the rules, de-legitimizing the rules, following regulations to absurdity, acting out subversive obedience or manipulating exterior compliance for the sake of an interior violation. Their dramatic condescension in formal submission, their duteous deference to nonessentials, their capacity to sap the strength of hegemonic aspirations, their ability to make relative adjustments to established policies, the parody of experts—the hustle, the shuffle, the ruse, and the con. These but scratch the surface of a repertoire which, indeed, must bring a doting smile to the face of God.

The other is overt, but for what it lacks in subtlety it makes up for in earthy candor and the four-letter exactions of primal Anglo-Saxon language. The perfectly timed flatulation, the capacity to embarrass, the coordinated use of odor whether of body or breath, and the capacity to undermine the exterior and pretentious ambitions of "saviors" by the wondrous ability not to give a holy damn: This is a short list. And then there is the story of that resourceful bum-of-a-man who like royalty opened his heavy winter coat, ceremoniously unzipped his pants and grandly urinated all over the desk of an imperious welfare worker.

No church or ministry in its right mind wants to be the object of such hard living strategies and tactics. Moreover, there is perhaps no place where the church runs the risk of alienating the hard living more than in its service and outreach programs.

Hence, we will look at the practices of these hard living churches to discover how they attempted to deal with these issues of control, protest, and resistance, while attempting—compassionately I believe—to be in genuine community with them.

Genuine Need

Without taking back a single thing about Marti Scott's comment on the importance of focusing on the capacities of hard living people in doing ministry, there is no question, and she would agree, about the fact of their very real needs. Pastors give significant amounts of time to meet these. What follows is an outlined summary with a few illustrations of what is a complex picture of services and activities. No church can deal with the realities of hard living without touching the necessities of their lives. At the same time, meeting needs must be done with genuine sensitivity to the issues of control, protest, and resistance. Practices commensurate with this sensitivity should follow.

Basic needs like food, clothing, housing/home renovation and maintenance, medical care, legal services, mental health, twelve-step are those most often mentioned by pastors and church leaders. Tim Barber, for example, coordinates a food program for thirty-six congregations. They receive reports of need and then provide information to congregations who make deliveries to people. Pat Morris has enormously amplified her ministry through grants and bringing other organizations in to work out of the church building. "We fed 91,000 people in this church last year, and we have a membership of thirty-five." While not all operate on this scale, virtually every pastor either provides some kind of food pantry or participates actively in some ecumenical and/or cooperative effort. Jane White-Stevens reports that occasional meals like

"Potlucks" are greatly appreciated. A lot of the hard living don't have good diets and like good food. A lot of them are singles, too, so that sometimes it looks like a singles ministry. The youth of her church also had a spaghetti dinner from time to time for which they charged a sliding fee, "so they put in what they can." In some instances the hard living "buy" food by providing three hours of community service in exchange for it.

Clothing, too, is mentioned by all. In most of the cases the clothing is sold at a minimal price. The pastors say that this kept it from feeling like charity and that the hard living seem to prefer it that way. Rexine Bryant added that giving clothes away will lead to abuse in her experience.

In some cases medical care is a major aspect of the churches' programs. The clinic at Rexine Bryant's church serves 1200-1500 people per year. They have medical doctors regularly giving their time, and they now have the capacity to go up to 2000 persons per year. Tim Barber's program coordinates with nursing services at a local clinic. Marilyn Gebert's church has an M.D. who comes to the church on a weekly basis and gives the medicine he prescribes. This became a well-child clinic. A dentist also makes visits to examine patients, and then takes them to his office for free dental care.

Legal services are made available in some of the churches, although not on the scale of food, clothing, and medical care. These services usually did not deal with criminal cases, but with divorce, custody, collection agencies, garnishment of wages, and civil suits. Typically limited to the geographical area around the church, this legal help is for people who need an attorney, do not have one, cannot afford one, and do not know where to get one.

Mental health is a serious concern in hard living settings. In some cases these services are offered in the church through outside agencies. "Pathways" is a program, for example, operating out of Rexine Bryant's church for children in homes where there is substance, psychological, and physical abuse.

Other churches provide counseling by the pastor and, also, by mental health specialists. George Miller has a counseling ministry that reaches ten counties and serves sixty to one hundred people per week. Much of his work focuses on single parents, support groups, parenting training, and on the co-dependency arising out of families with alcoholics and other drug abusers. Having been there for seventeen years, George believes that the intensity and scale of this work are now making substantive contributions to a small town that became economically depressed when it lost its two major industries.

Home renovation and maintenance, and housing programs in some instances are a basic service ministry. Sam Mann has been deeply involved in the building of new housing in his community, and Tim Barber organizes 500 volunteers a year to do upkeep and weatherization. Ron Roberts, who became involved in housing issues early on in his pastorate, now runs a personal business in addition to his ministry that does housing management. This is a continuation of his ministry, he believes. He originally got into it because he saw the need and because the extra income enabled him to remain for twenty-four years in the church he served.

A key question in all such service ministries is that of the potential for demeaning people in need. Nothing can raise the hackles of the hard living any faster than paternalistic charity. In such settings it is easy to cheer for hard living strategies of protest and resistance.

I find the pastors in these hard living churches, however, very sensitive about one-up, put-down "almsgiving." John Auer, for example, without my even suggesting the word out of our hard living interviews, talks about how important it is for the church to be "comfortable." He says, "We just try to be comfortable with reaching out." I got the impression that he wants this reaching out to have a kind of 'matter of fact' or 'taken for granted' quality in the best sense of those two phrases; that is, not to make a big deal about it. The church must not seem to place itself in a "superior" position. Rather its work and services are simply a part of what it means to be in solidarity with the community.

John discusses ten or twelve self-help and twelve-step programs that work out of the church facilities. "There is no proselytizing in these groups. The church just attempts to give off a feeling of being comfortable. We want to be around. . . . We try to give off messages of our commitment. For example, we have a Neighborhood Fellowship Feast for the people of the community and the hard living seem to feel most comfortable coming to this. It is a time when people in the church and in the community can have table together." This is a program where the hard living people both inside and outside the church help to prepare the meal.

In addition, John names other ministries in which the congregation attempts to be the church of the community: A feminist-lesbian coffee house, a minister to community life, a drop-in center in a house next door to the church, an open-door policy at the church itself, and an active advocacy and organizing role with the area. "But primarily," he said, "we as a church have a sense of call to this community.. We want to be identified with the community and its people."

Nancy Kaye Skinner had an interesting comment about the role of the long-time members of a congregation in making and keeping good relationships with the hard living. Having pastored two different churches that had been able to incorporate a dozen in one and a half-dozen of the hard living in another, Nancy speaks of the key role played by people in the church who embrace and care about the hard living inside and outside the congregation. Some church members give or find jobs for the hard living, others pick them up to take them to church and special events, and some just simply "help out." Nancy especially appreciates some of the older people in the church who had "a strong vision of mission and kept it alive. They would tell stories about poor people in the community, about people on the edges of the community, and about how these were really good people underneath. Just telling those stories tended to keep us humble and to remind us of what we were supposed to be about. . . . The storytellers were over sixty, and they were really important. . . . If you don't have a history—people telling the stories about people being down-and-out, but still being good people—you can't do it."

The solid work of individuals is not overlooked by Nancy either. She remembers one woman who would get up at 5 A.M., and make pies or buy rolls and visit people all day. "She delivered pies to people having trouble. Every week—without putting pressure on me or telling me what I ought to do—she would give me a list of all the people she had visited. She was wonderful."

Because of this witness, a group of women in their thirties befriended the wife of an alcoholic. These women then began to follow the example of this older woman. Subsequently, men in the church helped the husbands of these families with jobs, friendship, and support. Such witness made it possible to reach out and include people who otherwise remain outsiders.

The issue of "turf" is an important one. The church building must not be seen by the hard living as the possession of someone else but, indeed, that the church is *theirs*. What makes a building "comfortable" at least in part, was that it is "my church, too," not just "somebody else's."

That this is a real issue for many hard living people is an observation from Barbara Silver-Smith. She finds as others do that outside events—on the parking lot, out in a closed-off street—would draw hard living people in greater numbers than programs inside the building. These outdoor occasions are effective, apparently, because the hard living do not feel, says one pastor, "as likely to have the church get its claws into them."

The church where Dick Haddon serves takes the issue of "turf" seriously. Located in a Hispanic barrio with a fine physical facility, but with a declining membership, the church turned their educational wing over to the Hispanic community for a program called the Harbor Gateway Center, which serves people in the community around the church. A free lunch is offered every Saturday and a soup kitchen is attended by some two hundred. A program called Options for Youth obtains the names of high school dropouts and provides educational opportunities for two hundred fifty teenagers. They also have a class called "English as a Second Language" which enrolls nearly fifty people. In addition, Dick states that the center is a United Way sponsored program in an area that was designated by them as "underserved." The Center is now "multiethnic with a zoo of social services." This is an instance of a church turning over "turf" to a community so that it really is *theirs*.

Bill Robinson's congregation deals with this issue "up front" as he says, by including significant participation of community people on the board of the church itself. He reports that this is a very effective way to deal with the issues of turf and control.

As reported previously, it is also crucial that hard living people participate in providing services and in giving leadership to such efforts if a church is to be effective in dealing with the control issue.

Nancy Kaye Skinner points out that it also has to do with the fact that so many of them like "to give with their own two hands. Middle-class people tend to pay for things; the hard living like to *do* things *with* other people. If there's a work day, they want to be there." Pat Morris echoes this observation and underscores how much the hard living want to be an active part of both the leadership and the work.

We have already discussed how important it is for a program to work from and to expand and develop the capacities of people, and not just meet their needs. George Miller's church is the site of a five-day per week community program for senior citizens which serves four hundred to five hundred people. Each day has an in-residence lunch and all kinds of activities: sewing, games, bands, choruses, ceramics, health and exercise activities, meals on wheels, counseling, and so on. It is federally funded. Transportation is provided. This broad range of activities certainly calls forth the talents and abilities of these senior citizens and draws their vigorous participation.

SIX STRATEGIES

This selective and illustrative list does not, of course, exhaust the breadth of services and outreach programs conducted by these churches and their pastors. Much more could be said at this point. The even more important matter here is how these ministries are carried out so as to deal substantively with the issue of control while meeting very real human needs. The church leader can pursue six strategies.

1. The outreach and service ministries of the church most effectively respond to the issue of control by being offered "without strings attached."

2. Nothing can take the place of the church identifying with the people of the community so that the hard living find it a comfortable place where the church is in solidarity with them, indeed, where they *are* the church.

3. The long-time members of the church who are not themselves hard living have a central role to play in interpreting the latter as different *and* as "our kind of people." The practices of compassionate hospitality in contrast to demeaning charity are essential.

4. The issue of "turf" can be met effectively by the participation and leadership of the hard living on boards, programs, and missional outreach.

5. Practices indigenous to hard living lives and expressive of their styles bespeak the most genuine kind of hospitality and do as much as anything to break down dividing walls of disrespect and demeaning patterns of participation.

6. Without denying the spiritual and moral necessity of meeting the real needs of people a congregation will do its

best work when focusing on the expansion and development of the capacities of the hard living and opening
opportunities for their fullest expression.

While these six strategies do address the control issue
between the hard living and the church, and, while they may
provide appropriate ingredients for dealing with their protest
and resistance, they are not enough, especially with respect to
protest. The protest and resistance of the hard living come at
least in part, out of experience that is as wide in scope as the
entire society. It is not enough for the church to be a place of
hospitality and community, as important as these clearly are.
Our society presents the poor and the hard living with
systemic issues that cannot be addressed by inclusive
churches alone.

A desperately important ministry awaits the church in the
social realities that constitute poverty at the beginning of the
third millennium and which so destructively affect hard living.
Almost all of the pastors addressed this question, and some
were actively dealing with it. So we turn to the matters of
advocacy and justice ministries. Ministries of this kind open
up a profoundly appropriate focus for the protest and
resistance of the hard living.

ADVOCACY AND JUSTICE

Three of the Gospels (Matthew 26:6-13 and Mark 14:3-9)
report Jesus saying that we would always have the poor with
us. Some people seem to draw a comfortable complacency
from this idea. But two things need to be clarified. According
to the gospel of John (12:1-8) Jesus said this to Judas, *who was
about to betray him* and who was fault-finding against a woman
who had presented a precious gift to Jesus before his torture
and death. Do we really want to draw social policy from a
situation so constituted of the treachery of Judas, the
generosity of the woman, and the desolation of Jesus? Mark

even adds, "whenever you will, you can do good to them" (Mark 14:3-9 and Matthew 26:6-13).

Second, Jesus said we would always have the poor with us, but he did not say we would always have *systemic* poverty like that in the United States of America. Even in the best society, short of the Commonwealth of God, some people will be poor by virtue of their own indolence or their own absence of materialistic pursuits or, perhaps, because of an ascetic and servant vocation to God. We *shall* always have the poor with us, but no support is to be found in Jesus' life or the comment to support the structured social inequality that stalks the bottom twenty to twenty-five percent of this society.

This systemic question and others around racism and sexism are marked concerns for hard living pastors. Many of them voiced frustration that they have not been able to deal with such issues in more effective ways. Some are consumed by the pressures of pastoral work, and others found that they have little time left after fulfilling heavy demands on them for the provision of services and outreach ministries. Even so, a few have made genuine strides in this area.

Chuck Kallaus began his ministry literally on the streets working out of a storefront and funded by the First United Methodist Church in his town. Within five years he had moved to a larger storefront and then into a new metal building which housed his growing congregation with an attendance of one hundred fifty, two-thirds of whom were hard living and the rest senior citizens. "Advocacy was big," he says "people needed to know what they had a right to. We worked with the utilities and got a cold weather rule so that heat could not be turned off in the middle of the winter." The church is also an advocate with landlords of the people. "Some of them were members of First Church," the source of his funding initially. A good many of the pastors speak of the church or of themselves entering into dispute with the courts, housing authorities, employment practices, school issues, welfare policies and programs, health services, aid to families and children, police protection, and so on.

In some cases the churches and pastors are deeply involved in organizing. Marti Scott, for example, worked very hard for certain candidates for political office. This was cause for consternation with some members of her congregation. "During this time we had a fight over the American flag. It had been sent out to be cleaned, and some of my people thought that I had just removed it. As they insisted that it be restored to its usual place, I told them it would be, but I also maintained that as long as that flag is in this sanctuary, then I'm going to participate in the politics of this country."

Bill Robinson's ministry has broadened political organizing to the state level. "We have developed a network in each of the four congressional districts in the state so that the people of our community can identify their interests and go to work on them. Recently, he said, they have brought together eight hundred people from across the state to work on the politics of drug issues. We are trying to get others and we've got a lot of lay people who want to be involved but who are getting blocked by the clergy of some of the churches."

Bill's church is also deeply involved in a community development program which links the church and the community around issues. With a board that is composed of fifty-one percent of its membership from the church and forty-nine percent from the community, they are focusing on three major issues: public policy, drugs, and economic development. Funding for this program comes partially from the national denomination which requires that such a program be active in at least three of five areas which includes youth and violence, in addition to the three above. This board also has a 501-3-C status which makes it a private nonprofit agency and able therefore to receive funding from a variety of sources.

Marti Scott attempted to bring church-based community organizing into her area to deal with the issues of jobs and systemic change. "Very late," she says with regret, "we put together an economic summit where we used the information from *their* lives to talk about the economy as they saw it. I wish we had done it sooner." Her point was that this grass roots and

hard living experience of basic community economic issues
gave these questions, which are often abstract and distant, a
sharp focus and concrete relevance to their lives. Marti
believes that this approach has immense value and could be
widely used among the hard living to address systemic issues.
Convinced that hard living people have to empower themselves, she sees the necessity to do much more work in this
kind of organizing.

If there is a top priority of work where these pastors wish
they had more resources and could spend more time, this kind
of empowerment and systemic change around the issues of
poverty would be it. In most instances, these pastors are
simply overrun with raw human need that continually shows
up on the doorstep of their highly accessible professional lives.
The day begins and then suddenly ends having been filled by
too many clearly needed claims. The incessant wearing,
enveloping, immediate, compelling needs of people militates
against the time to plan, to organize, and to move on these
deeper, more glacial, and, of course, more fateful issues.
Moreover, the money, the competence, and the resources to
organize and empower are hard to come by in churches that
already operate on a shoestring and who work with people
who have nothing. In the face of the mammoth mobilization of
bias against the poor and the sheer weight of societal-wide
institutional drag, one would have to be crazy to be optimistic.

Still, faithfulness means believing in a vision not yet true
and holding on to a commonwealth that ever outruns our
constructions in this fate-filled world which has, nevertheless,
been promised salvation.

In the meanwhile, I draw hope from Second Isaiah, which I
have loved ever since I first heard it. It is post-exilic; it is written
as the people of Israel return home. It is, of course, the prophet
of hope, but a strange prophet. You will notice that the writer
does not speak of David's kingdom, he is not a proponent of
that royal theology. No, he goes back to an earlier time. Second
Isaiah declares that the way of the Lord will be prepared
through the wilderness. The prophet goes back to the Moses

tradition, knowing full well that faith is ever being born in the desert. For this reason he can declare that water will burst forth from rock, that the hills will sing, that the valleys will be exalted, that the rough places will be made plain, and that there will be a highway even where there is no path. Such is the promise to those in the desert. The wilderness, according to Second Isaiah, is the last place to give up hope. It is the place where God comes.

It is not my intention here, however, to solve the intransigent problems of poverty and the hard living by calling upon some divine intervention to bring history to a close in the next few years so that we can avoid the dismal prospectus and the hard work ahead. No, my contention is rather that the end of history in God operates in the interstices of our time in the here and now, and that the deepest hope is always born where there isn't any. Deeply related to this conviction is my sense that our direction with the hard living lies in a host of smaller churches all over our land caught in the stationary exile of having been left by the people who once were their members. In racially and economically transitional areas, in these wastelands abandoned by the affluent and the middle class, in these declining old neighborhoods in the city, and the languishing communities of rural America: here is the desert and here is the hope for the church's ministry to the hard living.

I find some congregations that have only twenty-five souls in attendance at Sunday worship, but a half-dozen or a dozen or more were hard living. And, yet, these kinds of churches may have ministries as creative and as faithful as any in their community. The wonderful thing about the hard living is that such places can be home; they can be "comfortable." I remind you, too, that the great majority of these churches are not "showplaces." They are not on the east or west coast; they are not the palaces of the kingdom. They are hard-scrabble, work-a-day congregations toiling in the desert looking for a highway nowhere in evidence. My guesstimate is that there are twenty thousand smaller churches in this land that not only can do this ministry but could make it their primary focus if they are to meet the needs of their publics, and if they are to do what is righteous.

Should these churches become places of compassionate solidarity with the hard living, should they become the experimental ground of ministry and mission with the poor, should they become a place to shuck the destructive rage and to focus a politicized anger as a work of love, it could make a significant difference. These churches, to be sure, cannot do everything, but they can be an important part of God's work with the poor and the hard living in the land. These churches can work together, they can share what they learn, they can organize within and beyond their neighborhoods. They could, indeed, be a focus for the protest and the resistance of hard living people. They could build, church by church, a network of political action made up of the hard living, who really know the score, to act on the issues so determinative of their lives.

Suppose you are a pastor or a lay person in a church that has hard living people in the community around your church. How does one begin? Let's get started.

10

GETTING STARTED

My wife and I eloped and came up to Indiana from Kentucky in 1951. I was not a Christian at the time. I had been in the military and had a lot of bad habits. I drank a whole lot. There was something lacking in my life, but I told her that if she would marry me, I would not drink again. Then, that same year the Lord saved me."

Quite frankly, I was actually afraid to call Chad Burkhart. He was the pastor of a Free Will Baptist Church, and I was apprehensive that he would simply dismiss me as one more left-wing, liberal seminary professor who had never been saved and who was not worth his time. I was not prepared really, for this warm-hearted, terribly decent, God-intoxicated, Jesus loving, down-on-the-ground, compassionate, humble man. I liked him so much that we talked an hour and a half, long distance, and it cost me fifteen dollars. I would have gladly paid ten times the price.

He went on. "There was a bunch trying to get a church started, and in 1954 the Lord called me to preach. I was the most unlikely person. The Lord gets all the credit because He took absolutely nothing and made me a preacher."

His humility grabbed me. I listened for any instance of pretension or some evidence that it was a form of reaction formation, a feigning of virtue in order to play the role of religious leader whose arrogance and self-seeking were covered by a fawning of self-debasement. It was not there. The longer we talked, the more ashamed I was.

"We rented a little ole building out in the country and started having church. Then God laid it on my heart that I was to start a church over in this small community in the poorest part of the country. Most of the people in my little church didn't want to do it, but I just had to. God had just burdened my heart with it. I couldn't do anything else. I just had to go."

I waited to hear how he would deal with this kind of split in the church, and I wondered if he would be able to take a nucleus of at least fifty to a hundred members with him. I knew he would need a base. You do not begin with nothing. After all, the man and his family had to have something. They had to eat, for crying out loud.

"Well, I lost half of my membership when we went into this new area, and we only had thirteen to start with!"

Chad has been there for thirty-eight years as of this writing. His church now has three hundred and fifty members with an attendance almost equal to that. Eighty percent of them came out of hard living, he says.

"Those people over there were just my people. We were kindred. I don't know. Ministering to people that come from that background. . . . It's just as normal to me as breathing. When I minister to somebody who gets drunk, crashes a car, and gets in jail, I know what that's like. I remember where I came from. I didn't pull myself up by my bootstraps. It was Christ. My people are the same way."

I asked him what he would do differently if he had it to do over again. "I would have accepted Christ much sooner, but other than that, I don't know anything I would do differently. It's almost that God led me everywhere I've been. Given all that's happened to me, only Christ could have led me."

I knew, of course, that such a ministry, even by so obvious a saint as Chad, could not have been without its problems, but before I could ask, he added, "It's not been all mountain time. It's not been all glory hallelujah, but I trust Him. If I'd been told

I'd love the Lord the way I do. . . . Well, I just couldn't have imagined all that's happened."

Later when I asked him how someone can stay in that kind of ministry for so long and still be so excited about it, he answered: "I may wear out, but I ain't gonna rust out."

None of the pastors was of one style or of one piety. Chad's humble, self-effacing warmed heart touched me, but I also admired the earthy, hard-nosed commitment of one of the women who described her early attempts to get started.

"I come out of a Nazarene heritage and with that one *must* have a personal conversion. Once that's happened to you, you have a deep and abiding care about people. I had a call to ministry early on and never seriously considered any other call."

I asked her how they got started.

"All we did was say we're gonna start. With the congregation I started with the sheep and the goats passage, and then I asked them: 'Where are you going to spend eternity?' I did cocky, bitchy, shit. I told them, 'I'll stay here if you go this way and do ministry with the hard living. If you are not in mission, you just need a care taker.' The congregation said: 'Let's do it.' "

Whatever the form of piety or the ways they expressed their spirituality, to a person these pastors expressed a deep and sustaining commitment to God and a burning sense of mission with the hard living. It is doubtful that anyone could carry on such a ministry without this touchstone of faith and dedication to the task. In a substantive sense, no one can get started otherwise, but still each of these pastors began with a certain concrete effort of ministry which will be instructive.

BREAKING OUT

Except for those situations where the hard living were already a part of the congregation, these pastors first had to make contact and develop a relationship. It will be helpful to look at these because, not surprisingly, there was a diversity of approaches.

Marilyn Gebert began by an intentional ministry to the unchurched. She called on them in the hospital, and she let it be known that she was ready to officiate at weddings and funerals for those who had no religious affiliations. Her ministry really began when she had the funeral of a drug pusher. The pusher had been to prison and was "very mean" when he got out. "But after I did his funeral, his mother, two sisters, a brother, and a niece began to come. They were then joined by a girl friend and her family."

A similar approach was reported by Rexine Bryant. Coming from a hard living background she held the funeral for a member of a Gunfighters Club. In talking about him she told the stories the club members had told her. With a one word change she quoted a line the deceased liked: "Though I walk through the valley of the shadow of death, I will fear no evil because I am the meanest son of a *gun* in the valley." The gathering roared in response, and Rexine said, "From that point on I was their pastor."

Several of the pastors began with the children. Patricia Meyers got a contract from the city to feed kids in the summer. "That got us going, we never looked back. We are now a million dollar outfit that never closes. After lunch we did nothing for the first two weeks. Then we did paper and crayons and asked if they would like to stay. Now we run Vacation Bible School on Wednesday for two hours after school. We have thirty-five to fifty elementary school children. Supper is at 5:30 P.M. and they go home at 6:00 P.M.

Chuck Kallaus started with the children as a way of also reaching adults. "We made friends with the children and passed out tickets for a free meal, a chili supper. When the adults found out we weren't going to be churchy, that we weren't going to ask them to give, that we weren't going to preach to them, they started to come. They didn't want to just sit there and listen. They wanted to talk, to be part of it and to say what made sense. We just tried to show we cared."

"My ministry started with the children," Al Lewis reported. "We started picking them up for church on Sunday. They started bringing their parents. I had been picking up the children, and one day this addict came out to meet me. I shared the gospel and he came to Christ. Now he drives the van and is the choir director. He wanted a new environment, and he's now a mainstay of the church. He became a spiritual leader."

Don Bakely was for twenty-five years the executive director of an inner-city community center known for its all-out commitment to the poor. To reach the hard living he always began with the youth. "If you can be straight with the teenagers, if the hoods trust you, their parents will get interested. You see, you represent real help to them, help to get their kids raised. It always worked best for me. But you gotta be straight with the kids. No b.s."

One of the pastors began at the other end of the age structure. George Miller took a hard look at his community and saw the large number of elderly there. His church released him to spend major amounts of his time with senior citizens. "It took seven years to establish that program. We were able to get federal and state funding. A lot of the elderly were Catholic. Most of them now feel they have a priest *and a minister*. Once that program was in place, then I turned to the young people."

Craig Hunter has had enormously creative ministry with the hard living. When I asked him how he got started, he told me that there was a group home across the street for people who had mental illness and some who were retarded. "We just visited them and told them that we would like to invite them to our church. They started coming. I don't know, it just seemed that when people in the neighborhood realized that we genuinely wanted the people from the group home, they realized that we wanted them, too, and they started to come. We were just 'up front' about wanting to be a neighborhood church, and we invited a lot of people. Then we began a lecture series that was topic oriented, like 'How to Talk to Your Doctor,'

'Stress,' 'Budgeting,' 'Depression.' Whatever seemed to be important to people, and they came. We must have distributed two thousand circulars to let people know what was going on."

Darrell Rickard remembered that his church's ministry to homeless men began with coffee and donuts. "Up until we started the program, we had to have a policeman on duty to protect the place, but not anymore." He wishes they had "the personnel and resources to do what I would really like to do." Their church has an active feeding program, a clothes closet, and the building is used as a place to get warm, especially on Sunday morning before the 10:45 A.M. service. These efforts have brought the active attendance of twenty-five to thirty of the homeless in worship and often more.

Bob Hodges is co-pastor with Darrell, and he reported on the formation of a Vietnamese congregation which has begun in their church and which is served by a local seminary student. Bob also emphasized the importance of the church as a drop-in place. "It can be dangerous for the older people out there on the street. They need a safe and secure place."

The point of all this is that there are many ways to get started. Virtually all the pastors intimated, if they did not say it directly, that the major question is whether the church really *wants* to be in ministry with the hard living. The means for initiating such a ministry are various it seems. The central issue is will and the commitment to see it through.

It is, of course, not easy for a church with a congregation of respectable lower middle-class people to open up to and identify with the hard living. It means change. So the pastors were asked about the conflict and trouble they encountered when these hard living ministries began.

CONFLICT AND TROUBLE

Most of the hard living churches are in transitional neighborhoods. These transitions are almost always of either class or race, and usually both. The neighborhood is moving from middle class or traditional blue collar to poor and from Anglo-European to African American or Hispanic. Changes of these kinds do not exhaust the options presently lived out in the United States, but they do raise most of the issues churches face when involved in such transition.

Conflict is ubiquitous in social life, and these churches were no exception, but certain issues are mentioned many times. First, issues of race and class and of racism and classism appeared frequently. Sometimes church members resisted the hard living because they were not "our kind of people." Sometimes church members used outright social slurs or called people "no good." Occasionally, they simply tell their pastors that there was "no place for those people in our church." Doubtlessly racist and classist fears affect all the churches to some extent, but perhaps the most overt conflicts take place around issues of hygiene and life-style. Cleo Coleman said that in ministry with the hard living "you have to get past two levels: the senses level and the values level. Once our church folks got used to people who smelled differently and dressed and behaved differently, we were all right. You've just got to get past these two stages."

The behavior of some hard living people could also be a problem. The conduct of children in worship is disturbing to old timers, but their parents shouting at them or spanking them during the service unsettles them more. One man in Ron Roberts' church who had a serious mental illness simply wandered around in the sanctuary during worship. He also sat at the front and often left and returned several times during the service. Many other issues surface around life-style questions: moral concerns, family practices, child rearing, work patterns, language, alcohol and drugs, and so on.

Some of the behavioral problems center around religious practices. Bob Metheny characterized the tradition of his church "as more liturgical and formal, but the hard living were more fundamentalist. They wanted a more literal interpretation of Scripture, more informality and spontaneity." Interestingly enough, he found that fundamentalist professionals and the hard living tended to agree on style of worship while the traditional blue collar long-term members were uncomfortable with this approach.

Many of the pastors point to the issue of power as a major source of conflict. Nancy Kaye Skinner, for example, observes that limits are placed on what the hard living could do. "They could come to church and Sunday school but could not take on a role or position of leadership in one of her churches." Rexine Bryant observes that "you don't have trouble if there aren't too many hard living people to form a voting block and challenge the power structure of the church." Rexine believes that the major problem is "around giving up power."

Conflict among the hard living themselves became a concern for Chuck Kallaus. He preached a sermon one day on loving our neighbors even when we disagree with them. One hard living member came to him after church and expressed appreciation: "I'm glad you said that. I was gonna punch Virgil out." Chuck said he often felt that "they were on the verge of riot any Sunday. The problem was to make peace, but a lot of the time we didn't know what was going on."

PERMISSION TO HIT

I was surprised that so many of the pastors reported little or no conflict around reaching out to the hard living. The reasons for this seemed to vary, but clearly one of the reasons had to do with the leadership given to the situation. For example, Cleo Coleman, who was a program director and not, strictly speaking, a pastor, said that they really did not have a whole lot of problems. She explained, "But when I went there, I was a mature woman: a strong, assertive, know myself, people-type person, and I knew what I needed to do as a mediator. And I used those skills. I played an important role as a bridge between the church and the people of the community. I could help them understand why a woman on welfare is unwilling to leave it and go to work for MacDonalds at the minimum wage and then lose all the services welfare provides. And they were with me."

Barbara Silver-Smith also spoke about the importance of strong leadership. Her congregation was made up of blue collar people whom she described as very "accepting of her and of ministry to the hard living. They [the congregation] see it [reaching out to the hard living] as evangelism. They want me to be the leader. They expected me to be the leader. They expect me to come up with ideas, and then they get in there and do it with me."

In his ministry with the hard living and in his experience as a national director of urban ministry, Seth Beverly found it easy to reach out to the hard living when moving from the base of an African American congregation. "There's more compassion in blacks because they've been through so much. When they see in the Bible things about 'you were slaves in Egypt,' they identify with that." Seth reported that panhandlers on the street know that blacks are a soft touch. "They are easier to get money from. Blacks don't blame the victim; they have compassion for the victim." Seth was quick to add that he did not mean this was some inherent racial characteristic per se. He clarified, "a lot of this is political. Whites defend privilege, etc., because they have it. Blacks don't have the privilege and so on to defend." He went on to say that "there is a great deal of tolerance in the black community because we don't know how to reject the behavior without rejecting the person."

Ron Roberts came back to the issue of leadership style when he was asked about conflict. "We had an unbelievable absence of conflict, but my children tell me I'm a past master at denial. I make it hard for people to get overtly mad at me. I detest conflict, and I do everything to nip it in the bud. It's hard for people to hit you when you are hugging them. More than that, it takes the fun out of it when you give people *permission to hit you*. I also give people permission not to like something. That really helps."

A creative approach that drew on the capacities and resources of the congregation was offered by George Miller. "We provide programs for both men and women in domestically violent homes. We also have a program for sexually abused women. I believe that we keep this from being divisive [with our long time members] by having projects that people can do to express thanks. People donate work, ceilings, lights, plumbing, air conditioning services, whatever they can do to express thanks. We don't expect it, but it's there and most people want to do something. These folks provide $10,000 to $15,000 a year in projects. This speaks to the congregation and makes them glad the people are around."

Several of the pastors reported that they had difficulty reaching out to the hard living in previous churches. Pastors like Al Lewis said that "established churches didn't want to be innovative." His answer: "I just started a new church from scratch. We've had no problems."

In other cases a church had a history of working with the hard living, and such ministry simply was who they were. It "came with the territory." Bernard Keels spoke of Everett W. Stevens, Sr. and his spouse, Mary, who began the Shaw Church and had a ministry there for forty-one years. Stevens had been delivered from alcohol, was baptized in a bath tub, and developed a ministry with the hard living in that church from the very beginning. Bernie added that "there is always a constant need to remind ourselves from whence we come. Some want to forget."

MAINSTREAM MEMBERSHIP

One issue that is involved in almost all of the churches is that of continuing to work with and manage conflict with the long-term membership. Most of these are respectable people with strong ties to the tradition of the church. They usually constitute its financial base and hold the reins of power. When it comes to getting things done, to providing that steady, week-after-week, self-denying institutional commitment, they typically make up the "shock troops" of most local churches. Relationship-rupturing conflict with them could readily terminate, or at least sharply foreshorten a pastor's tenure. If one understands that most of the conflict issues addressed above are profoundly involved in this relationship, one readily understands why it is so fateful.

One pastor talked quite candidly about how volatile ministry to the hard living can become when one's relationship to the traditional membership becomes strained and conflict-ridden. In this case, the pastor admits several serious mistakes that led to the termination of the ministry with the hard living and to the loss of her job. Part of the problem, it seems, was that the pastor and newcomers, including the hard living, turned in a charismatic direction, a turn rejected by the long-term membership. The pastor also believes that the old line congregation would not "buy into spirituality, that is, people who were touched by God and found power and were helped. Those who did not said, 'This doesn't look like a United Methodist Church to me. Why is she doing this?' "

The pastor went on to say, however, that she made a fundamental mistake when she did not work very hard in her ministry with the long-term, respectability-oriented membership of her congregation. She confesses, too, that she became a victim of her own dysfunctionality. "I became too wrapped up with two people and became dysfunctional because of my loss of perspective. I got emotionally involved, became co-dependent, and got addicted to them."

Another pastor, Marilyn Gebert, was quite clear about how crucial it was to keep an active and empathic ministry with long term members. "I spent a lot of time with them, with their problems and their concerns. I visited. I reassured them. I let them know how much I loved them. You've got to do it." She went on, "I gave a lot of strokes to the church people for putting up with a lot. The church learned to love those [hard living] kids. I did a lot of visiting with the respectables. I had a good secretary, and she often got upset. She would tell me about people who were hurt and angry, and I would go to see them and listen and sympathize. I also preached a lot about why we were there and that we were there to change that community."

"I remember one person didn't like the [medical] clinic. She wondered what we would do if we needed the space for a dinner or funeral. I told them we wouldn't do a clinic the day we needed the building." Marilyn also told them, and this is testimony to the strength of her relationship with the traditional membership, "that I wouldn't stay if we didn't do this ministry." This could mean an immediate exit for some clergy but not with those who have formed a deep pastoral relationship of care where the ministry with hard living people is seen as a central expression of faithful witness and mission.

In defense of conventional, respectable mainline church members, let me say how important it is to be in touch with their struggles. It is too easy for professionals in this society to dismiss such people. They are often local, territorially rooted, socio-morally conservative but politically moderate people who hold to traditional values. They are less individualistic and more communal in their lives. They are deeply suspicious of the new morality, and they have not typically been served well by "experts," whether in the church, the schools, or the wider society. Their fight for respectability is, in great part, a struggle for dignity, especially in a consumer society that prizes affluence, youth, beauty, style, optimism, leisure, partying, tight jeans, and sexually explicit expression. The world of the respectables is instead one of tight budgets, restraint of excess, the control of impulses, and a suspicion of 'good times' which derive from the proclivities of male sociality and the violation of traditional commitments to marriage and family. They know all too well that the vaunted life-styles of television commercials will land them in the trash can of financial and familial disaster in a New York minute. They know, too, that the society is made for the people with money, but they have nine to five on their hands and a million chores at home and church, and a list of do-it-yourself jobs that will never be fully completed.

They are often faithful people, too. They love God and see the gospel as an endorsement of their basic ways to cope with a world that is not their oyster. Life is no rose garden, and they know it at least as well as any specialist in the human and theological "sciences" and "humanities." They love their churches, and these may be sites of a contemporized ancestor worship. Sanctuaries, memorials, stained-glass windows in old neighborhood churches become sacred and deserve reverence. I am amazed at "enlightened" university and seminary trained people who somehow find the rightful and appropriate respect, for example, for Native American ancestral burial grounds and sacred places but have nothing but derision and dismissal for those of contemporary traditional people who represent the largest single life-style group in the United States. In my fantasies I dream of a nonviolent army of the hard living who possess a sufficient repertoire of primal Anglo-Saxon "critique" to describe the colonial arrogance of such "cosmopolitans."

It does not take much imagination to understand why the respectables, on the front end, are not enthusiastic about ministry with the hard living. Indeed, they have fought their whole lives to avoid such "disreputable, trashy, no good, undisciplined, immoral, addicted lives."

But these respectable people—not all, but a great many, certainly enough—love Jesus. They love their churches *and* they love their families. And here the testimony of the hard living pastors is encouraging. When these respectables see Christ in the faces of the people on the street, when they read the ringing testimony of the Bible, when a few of them tell the stories and keep telling them, when they see family in the hard living, when they fall in love with the children, when they understand the plight of a mother who loves her kids and cannot get away from alcohol, when they see a "bum" wash dishes in the church kitchen for the potluck that fed him and heard his story, when they get to know the flesh and blood pain of their lives, these respectables know how to care. They are better at making commitments *and keeping them* than any other group in the society. They will continue to show up week after week, year after year.

Yes, some of them rival the worst bigots in the society, the most sanctimonious of the self-righteous, and the most self-satisfied people in the world. But these are not the majority and when the best of the respectables get serious, these self-satisfied, sanctimonious bigots have a wonderful opportunity to change or leave.

What is clear, however, from this study is that the warm-hearted pastor who is empathic with and genuinely cares and ministers to the respectables will more likely find allies than enemies. Indeed, one will often find oneself following and not leading such traditional folk. But compassion and respect for the respectables are necessities for dealing with the conflict and trouble that sometimes attend ministry with the hard living.

FOUR SECOND THOUGHTS

In the course of the interviews there were three different questions that were intended to ascertain information that otherwise might have been missed. The questions were: what advice do you have for others about doing ministry with the hard living? What is the most important thing you have learned in your ministry with the hard living? And, what would you do differently if you could start over again?

Though the answers to these questions vary considerably, they are roughly of the same kind no matter which question was asked. The pastors offered second thoughts, suggestions about what they wished they had done or could have done better, and they took the opportunity to say some things they really believed. Each of the three questions received about fifty answers each from the pastors for a total of more than one hundred fifty suggestions.

I lift up four issues which received significant comment from the pastors and seem to be matters of central importance. The first, and the one that drew the most urgent comment was the need to take care of oneself. This was expressed in many ways. Several of them focused on the necessity of the pastor developing a sense of one's boundaries, to have a clear sense of oneself, and to set limits. Others said things like: "Take good care of yourself." "The doorbell always rings, so find some time for your family and yourself." "Take a day off." "Take all of your vacation." "Watch out for burnout." "Watch out for your own co-dependency and dysfunctionality." "Find a good support group." "Work hard on your marriage." "Make sure your spouse understands what the two of you are getting into." Much wisdom resides in this advice. Quite a few of the pastors said they had left hard living ministries because they had not taken these personal issues seriously. It is too easy to become so engrossed in such compelling work that one's health or marriage or ministry or even one's motivation for the work can be broken by a lack of self-care. A sustained, high level of ministry in a hard living setting demands rest, recreation, renewal, and time for family and friendship.

The second most often mentioned issue was that of the pastor's own theological understanding, spirituality, and faithfulness. I was touched many times by how faithful these people were. Yet, it was clear to them how key their relationship to God, to Christ, to the Holy Spirit was. It was crucial, for example, "to have a clear sense of your own Christology," to "believe that if you will follow God's will, God will open doors for you," that hard living ministry "is a calling," that one must "nourish one's own spirituality," "that we must wait on God's time," that "our basic commitment must be to the Spirit and not to the institution," and that "Christ is central to my ministry." It is difficult to exaggerate how basic such theological and faithful grounding is in hard living ministry. The work is so demanding, it can often be unrewarding or, at least, not overtly successful, it does not pay well, it usually has little or no status, it is exhausting, it calls for energy of muscle, mind, spirit, and sheer dogged determination, and it simply wears one out. As Chad Burkhart said, "it ain't all mountain time, it ain't all glory hallelujah." After thirty-eight years he would know. But even as I write these words I wish you could have listened with me to these men and women talk. It would have made you glad to be a Christian, to be a human being, just to share a society with them.

Something extraordinarily powerful is at work in these people, and even on their worst days—when in despair and cursing their churches, the hard living, and God—they know it.

Third, these hard living pastors also fail, and the most serious pastoral problem in hard living ministry, I believe, is the nurturing, development, and cultivation of leaders who can succeed an effective pastor when she or he leaves. A handful of the ministries to hard living people simply evaporated when the pastor or another religious leader retired or moved on. This problem needs serious attention of the most carefully considered kind. The heroic effort required to initiate, to develop, and to sustain hard living ministry deserves a better fate. Hard living churches and their leaders need to begin the preparation of leaders long before any pastor or other key person contemplates a move. The involvement of such potential leaders and their participation in an apprenticed role are utterly crucial. Five to ten years of work can otherwise disappear within months.

Finally, it was clear that hard living ministry simply must give attention to systemic issues, to empowerment, to social change, and to social justice. The ministry that basically provides band-aids fails to get at the sources of the infection, but social change is an exacting demand. The hard living, whose protest and resistance are so often limited to the strategies and tactics of the powerless, typically have little confidence that "you can beat city hall." Their experience is otherwise. The episodic and mobile character of so many of their lives, the lack of confidence in their own abilities, the sense of an impending weariness which comes from failed organizing and drenched hope, the questions of who to trust, the easy satisfaction that comes more quickly through an obscene gesture and a four-letter invective than the painful day-by-day building of power that presumes a future most of them never had: These are the recalcitrant angular realities of their lives. Perhaps it cannot be done in every place, but some *have* done it, and it is so right that this alone makes it worthy even of a faithful failure. I believe with these hard living pastors that God is at work in this ministry. This alone gives it sufficient reason of the church to invest its life. Preset limits cannot be placed on what God can do or what the hard living can do, or what pastors can do or what these wonderful churches can do who know they have to be in mission and who hang in there and are working yet. There seems to be a special place in the heart of God for people who are no people, for people who are refuse and garbage, for people who are trash. In the mysterious, alchemic divine economy, they become God's people. They are given new names, new hope, and a new commonwealth.

All over this land churches have the hard living just beyond their doors. A tough and demanding challenge awaits them full of frustration and pain and a lot of sleepless nights. Things they hold most dear in these churches for which they struggled all their lives to preserve may be "desecrated," may be put to purposes they never imagined, and may fly in the face of what earlier church matriarchs and patriarchs held sacred. At the same time, they will discover how powerfully God comes to us in the lives of the marginal, the excluded, and the disreputable. They will learn, too, of how radically authentic the gospel can be in disenfranchised lives. They will hear prayer in profanity, intercessions in the very words that take God's name in vain, and liturgies of hope and life in earthy protest and vulgarity. Scratching beneath this they will find a Christ where none was expected. For some they will find there the reason for their lives, the very purpose for which they were called into this world. In the beginning many respectable church people will find themselves in an alien land filled with strange and threatening people, but this new place filled as it is with monstrous challenge and foreboding hardship somewhere along the way becomes the land of promise and finally home, the home they never knew, but for which they were always destined. Right now we need twenty thousand churches to embark on this trip toward home.

How to Get Cussed Out

Don Bakely was the executive director of Crosslines, an inner-city mission program in Kansas City, Kansas, for twenty-five years. Before that he had pastored an inner-city church in Camden, New Jersey. He is one of my favorite raconteurs in the entire world. I had wanted to talk to him from the time I began the research, but I put it off. His stories have too much influence on me, and I wanted to wait until things were in place. At the very end I called him, told him my purpose, asked to take him to lunch, and set a time. Where? He suggested the Indian Springs Shopping Center, a place equidistant from his house and mine. Wanting to buy him a nice meal, I asked him what would be a good cafe. He took us to the cheapest hamburger stand in the mall, explaining that "eating is something you just do, Sample. You do it so you can do other things." I did not mind. Usually when I am around Bakely I lose a lot of money, not to him, but rather because he makes me give it away. I stay away from him all I can.

Bakely can walk into a room full of complacent church folks who have no real interest in the poor, and, after listening to him for an hour, walk out reaching for their checkbooks to give him money and asking what more they can do. He is a dangerous man. You see, he tells these stories, stories out of his own poverty, out of a ministry of forty years with the poor and out of a wealth of truck knowledge born of tough experience that is impossible to replace. Bald, earthy, profane in a sacred sort of way, he regales me with one story after another as I rake the unordered onions from a double-decker overcooked hamburger. The man embarrasses me because he makes me weep, and, trying not to let him see my eyes water, I damn near choke on this carbon-coated burden I'm now determined to eat. Bakely loves an audience. He knows he's on a roll, and he turns up the pace.

"Sample, did I ever tell you about Big Mart and Ella in the church in Jersey."

"Naw, I don't think so." I never tell him I've heard a story.

First, I like to hear his stories again, and, second, you may miss the story he remembers while telling you the one you've heard. But I really had not heard this one.

"Well, you see, we had a church in Jersey that was like some you've been studying, good people in them, middle class, not able to relate to the people of the neighborhood, and dying. I knew that I had to make contact, and I knew that the only way I could get to the parents was through the kids.

"There was this gang, tough boys, in the neighborhood: Big Al, Cobble, Matt, and Big Mart. Actually, his name was Marshall, but we called him Big Mart."

I love to watch Bakely when he turns on to a story. His eyes flash; his hands become a moving, jerking, gesturing dance; he imitates his people; he changes his voice and imitates their accents; and he watches you like a hawk. If there is *anything* Bakely can't stand, it is an unappreciative, unadmiring audience. I do not disappoint him. He continues.

"I just started getting to know these guys. They're pretty tough, but I wrestle 'em and I win. I was a strong boy, Sample, and I can still whip you."

I say something to the effect that I'll let him believe anything he wants so long as I'm getting information from him.

"Anytime you think otherwise, boy, just let me know," he answers my belittlement with the "threat" he *always* makes. His bluster covers a gregarious interest in people, and, normally, when he's not on a roll, I insult him, tell him I could whip up on his over-the-hill body anytime, but not today. Insult is basic to our expression of affection for each other. Neither of us has hit anybody in fifty years.

"These kids get to like me, see. They believe that maybe the preacher's okay. Well, one day I'm sitting in the office and I hear this loud argument outside. It's Big Mart, and he calls somebody 'a fucking bitch.' 'Oh, God,' I says to myself, 'the first day he's in the building he's calling somebody names.' About that fast, Ella comes tearing into my office.

"'Did you hear what that young man called me out there?'

"'Yes,' I said. You see, Ella is the matriarch of that church.

She's really a good person, but she's kind of straight, you know. But she's real power, and, damn, she is mad!

" 'Well, what are you going to do about it?' she asked.

" 'That's a good question, Ella,' I says, 'a really good question. But the real question is what are you going to do about it.'

"Stopped momentarily, and a bit exasperated she says, 'I guess I want you to go out there and throw him out.'

" 'Ella', I said, 'I've been working for six weeks to get him in here. You want me to throw him out the first day?' I just couldn't do that, but I'm thinking real fast, so I says, 'Ella, let me tell you a story. Let me tell you this story, it's a true story, and then I want you to go home and think about it. Don't say anything right now. Just hear the story, then go home and think about it.' Well, she waited.

" 'When Big Mart was a little boy, his dad came home one night in a rage and began to beat up Big Mart's mother. He became so furious and so violent that he brought the children into the room, closed the door and forced them to watch while he killed her. He then took a paring knife and cut her head off in front of those children. When Big Mart could not stand it anymore he broke for the door and got out, but when he reached the top of the stairs, his father threw his mother's head and hit him in the back pitching him down the entire flight to the bottom floor. It knocked him out, but when he woke up on the landing, he was lying on his mother's head. . . . that's Big Mart. He's the guy you met out there, the guy who . . . uh . . . called you that name.'

"Ella didn't say a word. She just turned and walked out the door. I said to myself, 'I'm in trouble. This is over before it starts.'

"She was back in twenty minutes. I was worried. I wanted her to think about it longer than that, but she walked over to my desk and just looked at me.

" 'Well?' I finally asked, not really wanting to know what I expected to hear."

She says, "I guess I am going to have to learn how to get cussed out."

"Sample, the ministry of that church began right there, right then."

SUGGESTIONS FOR FURTHER READING

PART ONE: HARD LIVING

The term "hard living" comes from Joseph T. Howell's excellent book, *Hard Living on Clay Street* (New York: Anchor Books, 1973). I have previously discussed hard living in *Blue Collar Ministry* (Valley Forge, Penn.: Judson Press, 1984), and *U.S. Lifestyles and Mainline Churches* (Philadelphia: Westminster/John Knox Press, 1990). Arnold Mitchell, *The Nine American Lifestyles* (New York: Macmillan, 1983), describes one life-style group as "sustainers" which is close to those herein called the hard living.

An advocate of the homogeneity principle is C. Peter Wagner, *Our Kind of People* (Atlanta: John Knox Press, 1979). For recent counter evidence see Lyle Schaller, *The Seven-Day-A-Week Church* (Nashville: Abingdon Press, 1992) which argues that pluralistic churches are more likely to grow because of the array of options they offer.

For a view of language as necessary but not adequate, see Jacques Derrida, *Writing and Difference*, trans. by Alan Bass (Chicago: University of Chicago Press, 1978) and *Of Grammatology*, trans. by Gayatri Spivak (Baltimore: Johns Hopkins University Press, 1976), but see his more recent playful and aesthetic use of language: *Spurs: Nietzsche's Styles*, introduction and preface by Stefano Agosti; drawings by Francois Loubrieu; trans. by Barbara Harlow (Chicago: University of Chicago Press, 1981) and *Glas*, trans. by John P. Leavey, Jr. and Richard Rand (Lincoln, Neb.: University of Nebraska Press, 1986). Derrida tempts me enormously, but I have chosen here to stay closer to Ludwig Wittgenstein's, *Philosophical Investigations*, third ed., trans. by G.E.M. Anscombe (New York: Macmillan Publishing Co. Inc., 1958). See Christopher Norris, *Deconstruction: Theory and Practice* (New York: Metheun and Co. Ltd., 1982) pp. 129-132, for a decisive critique of deconstruction and why Wittengenstein's appeal to "ordinary language is a more viable alternative especially in listening to hard living people. Compare also Joseph M. Incandela, "The Appropriation of Wittgenstein's Work by Philosophers of Religion: Toward a Re-evaluation and an End," *Religious Studies* 21, pp. 457-474.

To understand story as a more basic category than theory or explanation, see John Milbank, *Theology and Social Theory: Beyond Secular Reason* (Cambridge: Basil Blackwell, 1990). For a fine collection of articles which deal with story from a theological perspective, see Stanley Hauerwas and L. Gregory Jones (eds.) *Why Narrative? Readings in Narrative Theology* (Grand Rapids, Mich.: William B. Eerdmans Publishing Co., 1989). For a contrasting perspective see Sheila Greeve Davaney, *Theology at the End of Modernity* (Philadelphia, Penn.: Trinity Press International, 1991).

1. GROWING UP HARD AND HOUSEHOLD RELATIONS

See a fine discussion of the wide range of theories about poverty, which sharply critiques the "culture of poverty" and "underclass" views: Michael B. Katz, *The Undeserving Poor* (New York: Pantheon Books, 1989). Katz also offers a very helpful discussion of homeless people. See also, William Julius Wilson, *The Truly Disadvantaged: The Inner City, The Underclass, and Public Policy* (Chicago: The University of Chicago Press, 1987). Peter H. Rossi, *Down and Out in America: The Origins of Homelessness* (Chicago: The University of Chicago Press, 1989), is an important discussion of homelessness with suggestions for change. See also Michael Christensen, *City Streets, City People* (Nashville: Abingdon Press, 1988) and Charles F. Strobel, *Room in the Inn: Ways Your Congregation Can Help Homeless People* (Nashville: Abingdon Press, 1992).

One of the best resources on children, especially those in poverty, is The Children's Defense Fund. See especially *CDF Reports, The National Newsletter for People Who Want to Improve the Lives of Children* (12 issues per year). See also Marian Wright Edelman, *Families in Peril: An Agenda for Social Change* (Cambridge: Harvard University Press, 1987).

Some of the most sensitive and humane research and writing on children is by Robert Coles. See *The Moral Life of Children* (Boston: Atlantic Monthly Press, 1986) and *The Spiritual Life of Children* (Boston: Houghton Mifflin Co., 1990).

On the place of rituals of deference and demeanor, and of giving and getting respect in social class, see Erving Goffman, *Interaction Ritual* (Garden City, N.Y.: Anchor Books, 1967) and Randall Collins, *Conflict Sociology* (New York: Academic Press, 1975). See my use of these rituals in *Blue Collar Ministry*.

On male sociality see James Ault, "Family and Fundamentalism: The Shawmut Valley Baptist Church" in Ralph Samuels, et al., *Disciplines of Faith* (London: Routledge, 1987); Elmer P. and Joanne Mitchell Martin, *The Black Extended Family* (Chicago: University of Chicago Press, 1978). See also Jerome L. Himmelstein, "The Social Basis of Antifeminism: Religious Networks and Culture," *Journal for the Scientific Study of Religion* 25 (1986), and Rebecca Klatch, "Coalition and Conflict Among Women of the New Right," *Signs* 134 (1988).

My point in chapter 1 is not that a "culture of poverty" has a component of male sociality different from middle-class society; rather that male sociality is an issue throughout life in the U.S.A. It is simply more devastating for the poor and hence "hedged against" by women in their coping relations with other women.

2. THE DRUG WORLD AND THE REAL WORLD

Two major books from Alcoholics Anonymous are *Twelve Steps and Twelve Traditions* (New York: Alcoholics Anonymous World Services, Inc., 1981) and *Alcoholics Anonymous: The Story of How Many Thousands of Men and Women Have Recovered from Alcoholism*, third ed. (New York: Alcoholics Anonymous World Services, Inc., 1976). See also Ernest Kurtz, *A.A.: The Story* (New York: Harper and Row, 1988) and Nan Robertson, *Getting Better: Inside Alcoholics Anonymous* (New York: William Morrow and Co., 1988).

For a searing critique of the treatment of skid row alcoholics that is more than twenty years old but still relevant, see Jacqueline P. Wiseman, *Stations of the Lost* (Englewood Cliffs, N.J.: Prentice-Hall, Inc., 1970). For a view of alcoholism that takes the role of culture seriously, see Norman K. Denzin, *The Recovering Alcoholic* (Newbury Park, Calif.: Sage Publications, 1987).

For an important treatment of the impact of drugs on a transitional community see Elizah Anderson, *Street Wise: Race, Class and Change in an Urban Community* (Chicago: The University of Chicago Press, 1990). See also Edward H. McKinley, *Somebody's Brother: A History of The Salvation Army Men's Social Service Department, 1891-1985* (Queenston, New York: Edwin Mellen Press, 1986).

On drug abuse see Terry M. Williams, *Cocaine Kids* (Reading, Mass.: Addison-Wesley, 1989); Michael D. Newcomb, *Consequences of Adolescent Drug Use: Impact on Psychosocial Development and Young Adult Role Development* (Newbury Park, Calif.: Sage Publications, 1988); Stephen P. Apthorp, *Alcohol and Substance Abuse: A Handbook for Clergy and Congregations*, second edition (Harrisburg, Penn.: Morehouse Publishing Co., 1990).

For a social history of drugs in the United States, see H. Wayne Morgan, *Drugs in America, 1900-1980* (Syracuse: Syracuse University Press, 1981).

3. THE CHURCH

See "Spiritual Salvation: The Last Resort" in Jacqueline Wiseman, *Stations of the Lost*. David Halle's *America's Working Man* (Chicago: The University of Chicago Press, 1984) reports on the charge of hypocrisy by Catholic workers in the northeastern part of the United States. Stanley Aronowitz in *False Promises* (New York: McGraw-Hill Book Company, 1973) describes the failure of the church in its commitment to working people.

4. HARD LIVING SPIRITUALITY

Robert Schreiter, *Constructing Local Theologies* (Maryknoll, N.Y.: Orbis Books, 1985) has helpfully discussed the "immediate providence" of popular religion. Jose Miguez Bonino observes that the poor view faith against "a supernatural screen" and the middle class against "a subjective screen"; see *Toward a Christian Political Ethic* (Philadelphia, Penn.: Fortress Press, 1983). These are valuable and useful metaphors.

Note how Feuerbach's position changed from *The Essence of Christianity*, trans. by George Eliot (New York: Harper Torchbooks, 1957) to *Lectures on the Essence of Religion*, trans. by Ralph Manheim (New York: Harper and Row, 1967). See V. A. Harvey's insightful description of this shift in "Feuerbach on Religion as Construction," in S. G. Davaney (ed.), *Theology at the End of Modernity* (Philadelphia: Trinity Press International, 1991).

On Marx's view of religion, as opiate, although a protest against real suffering, see *On Religion* (Moscow: International Publishers, 1957). On the *lumpenproletariat*, see *Selected Works, I* (Moscow: International Publishers, 1958).

Michel de Certeau's *The Practice of Everyday Life*, trans. by Steven Rendall (Berkeley: University of California Press, 1984) is a fascinating study, especially his discussion of popular cultures and ordinary language.

See Barbara Ehrenreich, *Fear of Falling: The Inner Life of the Middle Class* (New York: HarperCollins, 1989) for a helpful distinction between vernacular and critical discourse, and for a sharp critique of professional language, pp. 258-260. See also on "critical discourse" Alvin Gouldner, *The Future of Intellectuals and the New Class* (New York: Seabury Continuum, 1979) p. 29.

5. A HALF STEP FROM HELL

On respectable churches and their members see my discussion on the cultural right in *U.S. Lifestyles and Mainline Churches*.

On the sect church see Troeltsch, *Social Teachings*. A huge literature has developed around this notion. A good introduction is H. Paul Chalfant, et al., *Religion in Contemporary Society* (Sherman Oaks, Calif.: Alfred Publishing Co., Inc., 1981). Howell's *Hard Living on Clay Street* has an interesting discussion of "settled living" (respectables), but it is not as sensitively humane as his discussion of the hard living.

See Linell E. Cady, "Resisting the Postmodern Turn: Theology and Contextualization" in Davaney (ed.), *Theology at the End of Modernity*, for a discussion of contextualization and three contemporary options.

On country music see Frye Gaillard, *Watermelon Wine* (New York: St. Martin's Press, 1978); Douglas Green, *Country Roots* (New York: Hawthorn Books, Inc., 1976); John Grissim, *Country Music: White Man's Blues* (New York: Paperback Library, 1970); Bill C. Malone, *Country Music U.S.A.: A Fifty-Year History* (Austin, Tex.: University of Texas Press, 1968); and P. Carr, *The Illustrated History of Country Music* (Nashville, Tenn.: Country Music Press/Doubleday, 1980).

On spirituals and blues see Charles Keil, *Urban Blues* (Chicago: University of Chicago Press, 1966); James H. Cone, *The Spirituals and the Blues* (New York: The Seabury Press, 1972). See also Pete Seeger and Bob Reiser, *Carry It On! A*

History in Song and Picture of the Working Men and Women of America (New York: Simon and Schuster, 1985) and Anthony Heilbut, *The Gospel Sound: Good News and Bad Times,* revised and updated (New York: Limelight Editions, 1989).

For a treatment of social interaction as a game see Erving Goffman, *Encounters: Two Studies in The Sociology of Interaction* (Indianapolis, Ind.: The Bobbs-Merrill Co., Inc., 1961).

PART TWO: WHAT TO DO

Indigenous ministry requires sensitive attention to ethnic diversities. These readings are introductory suggestions.

A very helpful book on the differences among African Americans, Asians, Hispanics, Native Americans, and Anglo-European Americans is D. W. Sue with chapters by E. H. Richardson, R. A. Ruiz, and E. J. Smith, *Counseling the Culturally Different* (New York: John Wiley and Sons, 1981). An interesting description of the differences between the lifestyles of lower class African Americans and middle class Anglo-European Americans is Thomas Kochman, *Styles in Conflict* (Chicago: The University of Chicago Press, 1981).

On Mexican Americans see Alfredo Mirande and Evangelina Enriquez, *La Chicana, The Mexican American Woman* (Chicago: The University of Chicago Press, 1979); Virgil Elizondo, *The Future Is Mestizo* (Bloomington, Ind.: Meyer, Stone, and Co., Inc., 1988); and see Ada Maria Isasi-Diaz and Yolanda Tarango, *Hispanic Women: Prophetic Voice in the Church* (San Francisco: Harper and Row, 1988) for a treatment of a wider range of Hispanic women.

On Native Americans see James O. Olson and Raymond Williams, *Native Americans in the Twentieth Century* (Urbana, Ill.: University of Illinois Press, 1984). See also Paula Gunn Allen, *The Sacred Hoop: Recovering the Feminine in American Indian Traditions* (Boston: Beacon Press, 1986) and William Brandon, *The Last Americans: The Indian in American Culture* (New York: McGraw-Hill, 1974).

On Asian Americans the best work I have found is in the journals. Dozens of articles have been coming out during the past ten years. My suggestion is a careful perusal of the *Social Sciences Index* (Bronx, New York: H. W. Wilson, Co.) in a central public library or college library. This will provide a more specific focus on the specific Asian American group. For a general though dated treatment see A. Tachiki et al., *Roots: An Asian American Reader* (Los Angeles: U.C.L.A. Press, 1971).

The *Social Sciences Index* can, of course, direct one to hosts of articles on various ethnic groups in the United States.

6. HARD LIVING MINISTRY

Recent books on urban ministry are quite helpful for pastors and laity. See Wayne Stumme (ed.), *The Experience of Hope: Mission and Ministry in Changing Urban Communities* (Minneapolis: Augsburg/Fortress, 1991); Eleanor Scott Meyers (ed.), *Envisioning The City: A Reader on Urban Ministry* (Louisville, Ky.: Westminster/John Knox Press, 1992); and Michael J. Christensen, *City Streets, City People: A Call for Compassion* (Nashville: Abingdon Press, 1988).

Robert C. Linthicum, *City of God, City of Satan: A Biblical Theology of the Urban Church* (Grand Rapids, Mich.: Zondervan Publishing House, 1991) is a fine reflection on urban ministry from a biblical perspective.

7. COMFORTABLE PREACHING AND WORSHIP

A rural and Appalachian perspective on expressive preaching and worship can be found in Paul Gillespie (ed.), *Foxfire 7* (Garden City, N.Y.: Anchor Press/Doubleday, 1982). See especially the chapters on "Pentecostals" and "The People Who Take Up Serpents." See also Jack E. Weller, *Yesterday's People: Life in Contemporary Appalachia* (Lexington, Ky.: The University Press of Kentucky, 1965). An interesting discussion of urban sect and cult movements can be found in Robert Lee (ed.), *Cities and Churches* (Philadelphia: Westminster, 1962), but it is too psychosocially reductionistic and pays inadequate attention to the religious and spiritual commitments of the members of these churches. A more sensitive treatment of a "sect-like" church is Nancy Tatom Ammerman, *Bible Believers* (New Brunswick, N.J.: Rutgers University Press, 1987). The classic treatment here is, of course, Ernst Troeltsch, *The Social Teaching of the Christian Churches*, 2 vols., trans. by Olive Wyon (London: George Allen and Unwin Ltd., 1931).

A grassroots view of preaching and worship in evangelical churches can be found in Randall Balmer, *Mine Eyes Have Seen the Glory: A Journey into the Evangelical Subculture in America* (New York: Oxford University Press, 1989).

Nicholas Cooper-Lewter and Henry H. Mitchell in *Soul Theology: The Heart of American Black Culture* (reprinted in Nashville: Abingdon Press, 1991) spell out "core beliefs" and their expression among African Americans, an extraordinarily helpful discussion.

See David Luecke, *Evangelical Style and Lutheran Substance* (St. Louis, Mo.: Concordia Publishing House, 1988) as a call for a more indigenous ministry in the Lutheran tradition.

On tacit understanding see Michael Polanyi, *Knowing and Being*, ed. by Marjorie Grene (Chicago: University of Chicago Press, 1969), but his work needs more development from a view that takes orality, story, proverb, and social class as its departure. I am presently working on this and hope to publish such a piece within a year after publication of this book.

8. NONLITERATE CHRISTIAN EDUCATION

See Walter Ong's superb work on orality, especially *Orality and Literacy* (London: Routledge, 1982), and *The Presence of the Word* (Minneapolis, Minn.: University of Minnesota Press, 1967).

See Donald B. Rogers, *Urban Church Education* (Birmingham,

Ala.: Religious Education Press, 1989); E. C. Roehlkepartain, *Youth Ministry in City Churches* (Loveland, Col.: Group Books, 1989); C. R. Foster and G. S. Shockley (eds.), *Working with Black Youth: Opportunities for Christian Ministry* (Nashville: Abingdon Press, 1989); Janice Hale-Benson, *Black Children: Their Roots, Culture and Learning Style* (Baltimore: Johns Hopkins University Press, 1986), and George D. Spindler (ed.), *Education and Cultural Process: Anthropological Approaches* (Prospect Heights, Ill.: Waveland Press, 1987).

For insightful perspectives on orality that have contemporary relevance see Teodor Shanin (ed.), *Peasants and Peasant Societies*, 2nd ed. (Oxford: Basil Blackwell, Ltd., 1987).

Steel W. and Priscilla C. Martin in their *Blue Collar Ministry* (New York: The Alban Institute, 1989) have a very useful discussion of less "printy" and more oral methods in ministry to working people.

9. PROTEST AND RESISTANCE

On the resistance of the powerless see de Certeau, *The Practice of Everyday Life*, for a powerful illuminating treatment.

A very practical discussion of church-based community organizing is Gregory F. Pierce, *Activism That Makes Sense* (New York: Paulist Press, 1984). See, of course, the classic of community organization Saul Alinsky, *Reveille for Radicals* (Chicago: University of Chicago Press, 1946). Gene Sharp's three part, *The Politics of Nonviolent Action* (Boston: Porter Sargent Publishers, 1973) is the best treatment of nonviolent social action.

See James D. Davidson, *Mobilizing Social Movement Organizations: The Formation, Institutionalization, and Effectiveness of Ecumenical Urban Ministries* (Storrs, Conn.: Society for the Scientific Study of Religion, 1985) which analyzes social movements on the basis of structural and resource mobilization approaches.

The research of David Wagner and Marcia B. Cohen suggests that local social movements can have a significant impact on low income people's access to material and nonmaterial resources. Differences and similarities between poor people's movements and middle-class movements are also examined. "The Power of the People: Homeless Protesters in the Aftermath of Social Movement Participation," *Social Problems* 38:4 (November, 1991). See also their excellent bibliography.

10. GETTING STARTED

M. Christensen, *City Streets, City People*, has concrete suggestions for initiating new urban ministries. Strobel, *Room in the Inn*, is a complete primer for starting an ecumenical ministry with the homeless in any town or city.

INDEX